Iran at the C

For Mary-Lou, Rahima, Samra and Amina

Amin Saikal

IRAN AT THE CROSSROADS

polity

First published in 2016 by Polity Press

Polity Press
65 Bridge Street
Cambridge CB2 1UR, UK

Polity Press
350 Main Street
Malden, MA 02148, USA

ISBN-13: 978-0-7456-8564-9
ISBN-13: 978-0-7456-8565-6(pb)

A catalogue record for this book is available from the British Library.

Library of Congress Cataloging-in-Publication Data

Saikal, Amin, 1950–
    Iran at the crossroads / Amin Saikal.
        pages cm
    Includes bibliographical references and index.
    ISBN 978-0-7456-8564-9 (hardback) -- ISBN 978-0-7456-8565-6 (pbk.) 1.
Iran--History--1979-1997. 2. Iran--History--1997– 3. Islam and state--Iran. 4. Iran--Foreign relations--United States. 5. United States--Foreign relations--Iran. I. Title.
    DS318.8.S24 2015
    955.05'4--dc23
                                                    2015011699

Typeset in 11 on 13 pt Sabon by
Servis Filmsetting Ltd, Stockport, Cheshire
Printed and bound in the United States by RR Donnelley

The publisher has used its best endeavours to ensure that the URLs for external websites referred to in this book are correct and active at the time of going to press. However, the publisher has no responsibility for the websites and can make no guarantee that a site will remain live or that the content is or will remain appropriate.

Every effort has been made to trace all copyright holders, but if any have been inadvertently overlooked the publisher will be pleased to include any necessary credits in any subsequent reprint or edition.

For further information on Polity, visit our website:
politybooks.com

Contents

Preface

The Islamic Republic of Iran has forged a unique system of governance and pursued an unorthodox foreign policy posture in support of this system. The two, in combination with one another, have landed the Republic with many domestic difficulties and foreign policy complications since its advent in 1979. Yet, the Republic has managed to survive all internal and external challenges in an oil-rich but highly turbulent region, where local sectarian and geopolitical rivalries and foreign power interventions have played a key destabilizing role. In fact, although surrounded by active conflicts, especially in Afghanistan, Iraq, Syria and Bahrain, the Iranian theocratic pluralist political order has proved to be more resilient than could originally be anticipated. Whatever one's view of the order, it is now grounded in solid structures, with sufficient resources at its disposal to deal with any domestic disorder or to defy foreign pressures, from the United States and some of its allies in particular.

However, this has come at certain costs for the Iranian people, a majority of whom would have expected to enjoy better living conditions in view of Iran's rich human and non-human, especially oil, resources. Many Iranians have grown to be critical of both their government and the West, more specifically the United States, which has subjected Iran to severe sanctions, particularly over the country's nuclear programme. Meanwhile, a fresh air of optimism has come to grip most Iranians in the era of pragmatist Presidents Hassan Rouhani and Barack Obama, both of whom have shown a marked desire for a possible US–Iranian rapprochement.

The Islamic Republic is now indeed positioned at a crossroads. Should its Islamic government under Rouhani succeed in achieving major domestic and foreign policy reforms, Iran stands to be a very important and constructive regional power – a power that could also help the US to be a more effective player in the Middle East. The signing of the landmark Joint Comprehensive Plan of Action or nuclear agreement between Iran and the five permanent members of the UN Security Council and Germany (5+1) on 14 July 2015 has now provided a unique opportunity in this respect. On the other hand, if Rouhani fails in his mission, either due to domestic and regional opposition, or because of a similar factor torpedoing Obama's efforts, Iran can be expected to remain impregnated with seeds of instability and its region to experience more volatility.

This short book is grounded in my accumulative study of Iranian politics and society, as well as its regional landscape, over a long period of time. I owe much to so many people and institutions in the region and beyond. I cannot mention all of them, as some would not want to be publicly identified. However, it would be remiss of me not to register my sincere thanks to all of them, whether in Iran or elsewhere. Beyond this, I am deeply indebted to my very able research assistant, Stephanie Wright, whose help from the University of California, Santa Barbara, where she is a graduate student, has been instrumental in enabling me to complete this book. I am also thankful to another very bright graduate of the Australian National University (ANU), William Jenkins, who has developed an admirable knowledge of Persian language and Iranian society, for reading the final draft of the manuscript. Similarly, I am grateful to Dr Zahra Taheri for her advice, especially in relation to Iranian history, and to Louise Knight for encouraging me to write this book and to her Polity team, particularly Pascal Porcheron, for handling the logistics of the project.

Further, I must thank past and present professional staff of the Centre for Arab and Islamic Studies (the Middle East and Central Asia), of which I am the director, at the ANU. In this regard, I must mention Kerry Pert, Carol Laslett, Leila Kouatly, Lissette Geronimo, Pamela Lourandos and Anita Mack.

Finally, I owe a world of gratitude to my life partner and friend, Mary-Louise Hickey, whose love and support have made her a rock in whatever I do. As for my three lovely daughters, Rahima, Samra and Amina, they always remain the best I could ever wish for in life.

Note: In this book, the terms *jihadi* and *ijtihadi* are used strictly as they are described in the context of Iranian politics, with the first denoting revolutionary/traditionalist/conservative, and the latter meaning reformist/internationalist.

Amin Saikal
Canberra, July 2015

Abbreviations

ACC	*Majma-e Ruhaniyun-e Mobarez* [Assembly of Combative Clerics]
AIOC	Anglo-Iranian Oil Company
CENTO	Central Treaty Organization
CIA	Central Intelligence Agency
FBI	Federal Bureau of Investigation
GCC	Gulf Cooperation Council
GDP	gross domestic product
IAEA	International Atomic Energy Agency
IRGC	*Sepah-e Pasdaran-e Enqelab-e Islami* [Islamic Revolutionary Guard Corps]
IRP	*Hezb-e Jomhuri-ye Islami* [Islamic Republican Party]
IS	Islamic State
ISIL	Islamic State of Iraq and the Levant
NAM	Non-Aligned Movement
NPT	Nuclear Non-Proliferation Treaty
OPEC	Organization of the Petroleum Exporting Countries
SAC	*Jame'eh-ye Ruhaniyat-e Mobarez* [Society of Combatant Clerics]

Abbreviations

SAVAK	*Sazeman-e Ettela'at va Amniyat-e Keshvar* [Organization of National Information and Security]
UN	United Nations

1

Introduction

In December 1977, US President Jimmy Carter delivered a speech in Tehran in which he praised the country's close relations with his own. He described the oil-rich, pro-Western monarchical Iran as 'an island of stability in one of the more troubled areas of the world'. He attributed this stability to the 'great leadership of the Shah', stating, 'this is a great tribute to you, Your Majesty, and to your leadership and to the respect and the admiration and love which your people give to you'.[1] As it turned out, President Carter spoke too soon about the Western-backed autocrat Mohammad Reza Shah Pahlavi. Little more than a year later, the Shah was overthrown in the mass revolution of 1978/79 that gave rise to Ayatollah Ruhollah Khomeini's Islamic government, and a new Iran with an anti-American and anti-Israeli posture.

Contrary to expectations, the predominantly Shi'a Islamic Republic of Iran has continued to function as a relatively stable and secure state in an increasingly turbulent region. It has done so despite myriad and mounting domestic and foreign policy complications and challenges, arising partly from the nature of its regime and partly from its adversarial relations with the United States. Iran's current trajectory points to a future in which the Islamic Republic is unlikely to be any less significant than in its past. The Islamic Republic appears resilient and mature enough to uphold Iran's place as the inheritor of a rich civilization and culture, with a capacity in the modern age to act as a critical player in its region and on the world stage.

Since the revolution, the Islamic Republic has shown its capacity for survival against remarkable trials. Not least of these was the 1980–88 Iran–Iraq War, which was imposed on Iran by the Sunni Arab Iraqi dictator, Saddam Hussein (1979–2003). This proved to be the longest, bloodiest and costliest war fought in the modern history of the Middle East. Meanwhile, the Islamic Republic has weathered both the US policy of containment, which involved the threat of regime change and military action, and severe sanctions, backed by some of America's allies. It has also endured a number of highly destabilizing developments around it, ranging from the 1979 Soviet invasion and decade-long occupation of Afghanistan, to the 1991 first Gulf War between the US-led coalition and Saddam Hussein's Iraq over the Iraqi invasion of Kuwait, and the US-led interventions in Afghanistan and Iraq in 2001 and 2003 respectively.

The Islamic Republic has also had to cope with growing apprehension from a number of Gulf Arab states, led by Saudi Arabia; the 2006 war between Israel and the Iranian-backed Hezbollah in Lebanon; and the ongoing crisis besetting Iran's ally, the Syrian regime of Bashar al-Assad, since 2011. The latest episode that has confronted Iran, the region and the West is the rise of the Sunni extremist group of the Islamic State of Iraq and the Levant (ISIL) and its proclamation of an 'Islamic State' – IS – (*khilafat*) in June

2

2014. This – together with the subsequent US-led military campaign to destroy IS, thereby helping Iraq to preserve its territorial integrity and, at the same time, hastening the fall of the Assad regime – has generated a new conflict on Iran's doorstep. Iran has had to deal with this in ways that could both remove the threat of IS on the one hand and preserve its regional geopolitical and strategic interests on the other.

Throughout its existence, the Islamic Republic has endured a difficult journey. In many ways, this has been the fate of Iran since its consolidation as a distinct political and territorial actor more than 2,500 years ago. However, the period since the advent of Khomeini's Islamic government has been characterized by a degree of exceptionalism: it is the first modern Iranian political order to have locked horns with a superpower like the United States and thus to have challenged the prevailing international system.

The Islamic Republic has proved to be more enduring, with a capacity to rebound, than some foresaw when it came to power. Indeed, in the early days of the regime, when Washington rejected it as contrary to US interests and as an anomaly in the international order, some specialists and policymakers seriously doubted its long-term chances of survival. Yet, these doubts have proved as ill-founded as President Carter's praise of the Shah.

The resilience of the Islamic Republic can be attributed to a number of factors, with three worthy of special attention. The first is related to the nature of Iran's unique pluralist Islamic political order, as defined by Khomeini's Shi'a version of Islam. Khomeini and his zealous followers melded religious traditions and Islamic and nationalist ideas into a complex and at times contradictory framework in order to establish

3

a two-tiered system of Islamic governance that is now firmly entrenched. One tier was premised on the 'sovereignty of God', personified in *velayat-e faqih* (the Guardianship of Islamic Jurists, possibly in the tradition of the Aristotelian 'philosopher king' or figures like Khomeini himself), who is endowed with supreme religious and constitutional authority over the polity. The other tier was designed to reflect the 'sovereignty of people', represented by an elected President and National Assembly (*Majles*). The system of governance that evolved from this may best be described as theocratic political pluralism.

Khomeini's framework and approach to building this system, which have largely governed Iran's domestic and foreign policy operations to the present day, have provided the Iranian political system with a degree of inbuilt Islamic-based political pluralism. Over time this has spawned various Islamic factions, with three at the forefront: conservative, pragmatist and reformist, with each multifaceted from within. Although the system from the beginning weighed heavily in favour of the conservative faction, it has nonetheless contained space for the other two factions to gain political ascendancy from time to time through the electoral process in order to make the Islamic government and its foreign policy postures more palatable to the government's domestic and international audience. The election to the presidency of Hashemi Rafsanjani (1989–97) as the head of the pragmatist group, Mohammad Khatami (1997–2005) from the reformist camp, and moderate Hassan Rouhani (2013–) with the backing of both the pragmatist and reformist factions, is indicative of this function of the Iranian political and factional system.

This is not to claim that factionalism has not fragmented the ruling clerical elite and resulted in bitter

4

power struggles, as was the case over the disputed outcome of the 2009 presidential election. Nor is it to assume that the system of governance functions efficiently and effectively. To the contrary, the system suffers from serious internal stresses and tensions as well as patronage, corruption and dysfunctional features – the system's two tiers have grown increasingly incongruous. However, notwithstanding the state's coercive powers, the system has a measure of internal elasticity that enables it to engage in processes of reformation when necessary in order to cushion itself against internal discontent and foreign pressure. As such, whatever one's view of this system, it appears to have built more enduring structures of survivability than had the Shah's autocratic rule.

The second factor concerns the opportunities that have become available to the Iranian Islamic regime as a result of outside actors' – especially from the United States – policy behaviour towards Iran and its region. Washington's original rejection of the Islamic regime and its effort to contain it over the years ultimately proved to be short-sighted. Although the regime has long proved itself resilient enough to overcome or defy the US's adversarial efforts, President Barack Obama (2009–16) became the first American leader to recognize the futility of the US policy of containment. He has not only acknowledged America's past hegemonic interference in Iran, but also promoted diplomacy as the first instrument to deal with Tehran, especially since Rouhani's rise to power. With Iran's nuclear programme becoming a defining issue in the country's relations with the US and its allies, both sides finally succeeded in signing the 14 July 2015 Joint Comprehensive Plan of Action (hitherto called 'nuclear agreement') for settling the matter as a possible prelude to some kind of rapprochement.

The third factor is that despite Tehran's strong and publicly Islamic ideological stance, its foreign policy is driven largely by pragmatic rather than idealistic considerations. It has often relied on its ideological disposition as a source of policy justification rather than as a policy guide. A glance at the Islamic government's foreign policy behaviour from the early years of the revolution clearly indicates that the regime has been very calculating in most of its foreign policy moves. It has made sure that they are conducted more or less in proportion to the changing domestic needs and regional and international environments. This has been as much the case with its on-again/off-again hardline stance against the United States as it has been in the conduct of its relations with regional states and beyond. It has rarely failed to make necessary foreign policy adjustments, albeit on a proportionate scale, when these have been required by changes in Iran's domestic conditions as well as regional and international settings.

At times the Islamic Republic has given ground and at other times it has retreated, depending on the realities of the moment and the nature of the issues at hand, without appearing to make too many compromises that could render its Islamic ideology obsolete as an instrument of national legitimation and mobilization. There are many examples that illustrate this point. Major ones include Tehran's acceptance of an unconditional ceasefire in the war with Iraq in 1988; its neutrality over the US-led military campaign to reverse the 1990 Iraqi invasion of Kuwait; its acceptance of United Nations (UN) mediation to avoid a war with the Pakistan-backed Taliban over the militia's killing of 11 Iranian consulate staff in northern Afghanistan in 1998; its decision to back America's overthrow of the Taliban regime and to play a helpful role in support of American efforts to establish the Hamid Karzai government to replace that of the Taliban in 2001; and its decision not to create obstacles to the 2003 US-led invasion of Iraq. Lately, it has also included Tehran's refraining from direct confrontation with Saudi Arabia over the latter's 2012 military deployment in the Shi'a majority- but Sunni minority-ruled Bahrain and the Saudi-led military operations against the allegedly Iranian backed Shi'a Huthis in Yemen. Further, it has encompassed Rouhani's conciliatory endeavours in securing a resolution of the nuclear impasse with the United States and its allies as a precondition for ending Western and international sanctions. Even in the current Iraqi crisis, Tehran has adopted a posture that largely coincides with that of the United States in confronting IS.

At the same time, Tehran has not hesitated to exploit favourable situations when available in order to boost its soft and hard power in pursuit of strengthening its regional influence, mainly for defensive purposes. It has managed, largely through proxy operations, to build strong leverages by cultivating close relationships with either governments or subnational forces in the region – from Afghanistan to Iraq to Syria to Lebanon and Palestine. These relationships are not all of a security and military nature. Many of them also have serious political, economic, trade, cultural and humanitarian dimensions. The Iranian model of Shi'a Islamic governance has had little or no attraction in the Sunni-dominated region, but Tehran's policy actions have helped it to become an important regional player.

In spite of its international isolation, the Islamic government has also succeeded in building its hard power. Certainly, Iran's full military capability has not been tested since the end of the Iran–Iraq War. Also, by all accounts, the country's military machine and security

7

forces have not acquired an amount of technological and firepower capability to match, for example, that of Israel. However, Iran is not a pushover either. It has apparently achieved a level of military organizational and fighting capability whereby, in conjunction with Tehran's proxy forces and soft power activities in the region, an attack on Iran would be very costly for its perpetrators. Its security forces, some of which are the largest in the Middle East, are vigorously trained – both militarily and ideologically – and equipped to act as the 'guardians' of the Islamic government and the Islamic Republic. They are heavily schooled to dispense loyalty to the Supreme Leader and act steadfastly against any internal disorder and foreign aggression.

President Obama is persuaded that diplomacy is the best means by which to settle US–Iranian differences, and to deal with Iran's Islamic government. In this, he has overridden serious objections on the part of his detractors in the US and the region. He has resisted pressure from the forces of the right in the United States and Israel, which have persistently opposed any peaceful settlement that could normalize US–Iranian relations. He has also brushed aside concerns of a perceived Iranian threat from Saudi Arabia and some of its Gulf Cooperation Council (GCC) partners. The opposition to Obama's moves has been echoed in Iran, where Rouhani has his own powerful hardline factional opponents, with strong vested interests in maintaining the status quo. These opponents have been wary of the consequences of Rouhani's efforts to reach a lasting settlement of Iran's nuclear programme and other differences with the US.

There is no guarantee that either Obama's approach, or Rouhani's equivalent need to improve relations with the United States, will result in anything substantial.

However, should the nuclear agreement provide a major breakthrough leading to a US–Iranian rapprochement, it could produce the reverse effect of what the Gulf Arab states and Israel currently fear. It could result in less volatility and more stability in the region; possible US–Iranian cooperation could seriously assist the resolution of a number of deep-seated problems in the region.

Irrespective of one's view of the Iranian Islamic regime's domestic and foreign policy shortcomings, its Islamic government is now well entrenched, and has in the final analysis proved to be a widely responsible and shrewdly calculating player, not an irrationally fundamentalist one as has often been portrayed in the West. Given the state of turmoil in the Middle East, and given the Islamic Republic's influential position within the region, the US and its allies have ultimately been confronted with two choices: either to isolate or to engage the Iranian regime. The best option is to engage it and through this help the moderates and anti-extremists within what is essentially a pluralist ruling clerical stratum to succeed in achieving their reformist agenda, as currently advocated by Rouhani. In the present regional climate, Iran is a relative island of stability and any attempt to keep it isolated could only leave the region with more turmoil and destruction.

Purpose and structure

This concise book has two primary objectives. One is to explain and examine the transformation of Iran from a pro-Western monarchy under the Shah to an Islamic Republic, with a unique and, as some might argue, odd system of Islamic governance, under Khomeini and his successor, Ayatollah Ali Khamenei. It does so in the context of Iran's changing domestic situation and regional/global circumstances. The second is to look at some of the salient issues underpinning the Iranian Islamic government's policy behaviour as well as factors and trends that point in the direction that the Islamic Republic of Iran is likely to take in its internal and external dispositions in the foreseeable future.

The idea of writing this book did not originate with a view to providing a comprehensive account of Iran's domestic politics, national development and foreign relations in both historical and contemporary aspects. This task has been performed in a number of other books by some distinguished scholars of Iranian studies, whose works, together with some of my own, have been used as valuable sources of information and analyses in this book. In a nutshell, this book is penned with the specific objective of providing a monograph that is short, to the point and accessible to a wide range of readers interested in understanding as briefly as possible the main features of the Islamic Republic of Iran in its domestic and foreign policy operations in the context of the dynamics of relevant changes in regional and international situations.

While certain relevant theoretical tools and concepts are deployed to unpack the complexity of the Iranian Islamic government and its ideological and policy behaviour, the book is not designed to unfold or shed light on any new theoretical discourse. Nor is it conceived to examine Iranian politics and foreign relations within or against a particular theoretical/conceptual framework. In large part, the book essentially seeks to highlight those features of Iran's Islamic system and the country's foreign policy complexities that can inform us in relation to three questions: what has made the Iranian Islamic order tick? What has enabled Iran's

Introduction

Islamic government to survive against the odds, including severe US-led sanctions and bouts of international isolation? And what is likely to influence the Republic's future direction?

In the process, the emphasis of the book is more on the present and recent, rather than distant, past. It focuses a great deal on examining Rouhani's moderate, reformist agenda and his chances of success in achieving this agenda in the context of domestic and external challenges and opportunities confronting his administration. As part of this, his economic reforms and negotiations with the United States to secure a resolution of the dispute over Iran's nuclear programme and improve relations with the US are given primacy.

The book is divided into six chapters. After providing a brief historical background, the second chapter deals with Iran's transition from a secular pro-Western monarchy to an Islamic Republic as the outcome of a mass revolution originally spearheaded by the secular ideological and political opponents of the Shah. The third chapter covers the evolution of the Iranian Islamic political system as a complex and unusual phenomenon under Khomeini and his successor. Rouhani's election to the presidency on a platform emphasizing moderation and reform, in the context of joint efforts between him and Obama to secure a resolution of Iran's controversial nuclear programme, as well as the wider regional dynamics in which the current US–Iranian thaw has emerged, are examined in the fourth chapter. The fifth chapter focuses on identifying the factors and trends that could influence the direction of the Islamic Republic of Iran in the coming years, and the sixth chapter draws together the main conclusions of the book.

2

From Empire to Islamic Republic

For more than 2,000 years, the inhabitants of the Iranian plateau across Central and West Asia have viewed their multiethnic land as a cradle of culture and civilizational richness. In the words of the celebrated Persian-speaking poets Abul-Qasim Ferdowsi and Nezami Ganjavi:

> Iran is my land, and the whole world is under my feet.
> The people of this land are the possessors of virtue, art and bravery. They have no fear of roaring lions. Iranians are free-spirited, virtuous, and possessors of goodness. They are not terrified of evil forces.[1]

> All the world is like one body, and Iran like its heart,
> I, the speaker of this, do not shy from this comparison,
> Such that Iran is the heart of the world,
> It is certain that the heart's value is more than the body.[2]

These words by two literary giants from the past depict the essence of the thinking of a majority of Iranian people about their homeland, regardless of ethno-tribal and sectarian designations. In Ferdowsi's and Nezami's praises, Iran, or Persia as it has been known in the West (both names are derived from different Aryan tribes of Indo-European origins that settled in the plateau around 600 BC), is described as a fountain of knowledge and enlightenment and the source of those temporal and heavenly values and virtues that befit humanity and worldly existence. These two towering figures of classical Persian poetry exalt Iran as a land of such natural beauty, plenty and geostrategic significance as to make it not only the central pulse but also the envy of the world. Their description of Iran has subsequently been reinforced by many other Iranian literary figures, ranging from Abu-Muhammad Muslih al-Din Saadi Shirazi (AD 1210–1291), Khwaja Shams-ud-Din Muhammad Hafez-e Shirazi (AD 1325–1390), Nima Yooshij (AD 1895–1960), Mehdi Akhavan Sales (1928–90), Simin Behbahani (1927–2014) and Alireza Shoja'pour (1947–). The glory of the past has been no less inspiring to contemporary Iranian political rulers, including those who have governed the country under the banner of Islam since the Iranian revolution of 1978/79.

Iran before Islam

Iranians have good reason to take enormous pride in their pre- and post-Islamic history. Iran was the birthplace of many great empires and ancient civilizations long before the arrival of Islam in the mid-seventh century. The Iran-centred Achaemenid Empire (550–330 BC), founded by Cyrus the Great, stretched from Central Asia to the Balkans and North Africa. It was one of the largest and most advanced multiethnic and multicultural empires ever to be seen in the ancient world.[3] Hailing from the Parsu or Perses tribe of Aryan origin, Cyrus distinguished himself not only as

13

a great strategist and conqueror, but also as the instigator of what has since been claimed to be the first Charter of Human Rights, providing for the humane treatment by Iranians of the conquered inhabitants of Babylonia, and constituting also one of the earliest codes of international warfare. He established an elaborate administrative system of governance for his vast empire, patronized many cultural and social innovations, and promoted tolerance and justice among his subjects. After the Achaemenids met their ruin at the hands of Alexander the Great and following the latter's death in June 323 BC, the pre-Islamic Iranians built two other long-lasting empires after the demise of Alexander's successor empires: the Parthian Empire (250 BC – AD 255) and the Sassanid Empire (AD 224–651). Both of these empires more or less emulated the achievements of the Achaemenids in reinforcing a continued sense of uniqueness among the Iranians about themselves and the place of their land in the world.

The arrival of Islam

The defeat of the Sassanids by the Arab-Islamic armies in AD 651 resulted in the spread of Islam into Iran, but not in an enduring Arab occupation of its heartland or its vast Central and West Asian extent. Although a majority of Iranians in time embraced Sunni Islam in the place of Zoroastrianism, which had emanated from Iran and had hitherto been amongst the world's largest and most influential religions, Arab rule was nevertheless resisted and eventually repulsed. Islam was thus grafted onto an already solidified Iranian identity and indigenized culture and outlook.[4] The Iranians melded their pre-Islamic heritage with their new faith to shape and influence Islam in ways that did not eradicate their pre-Islamic legacy. Under various dynastic rulers, the institution of the *Shahanshah*, or 'King of Kings', accompanied by an increasingly refined but centralized system of governance that enforced the Shah's absolute rule, continued to be pivotal to the operation of Iranian politics and society for centuries to come.

European incursions

From the start of the sixteenth century, the Safavid dynastic rulers (AD 1501–1736), who hailed from Isfahan (nicknamed *Nesf-e Jahan* or 'half the world') and who turned that city into a majestic centre of political power, trade, art and culture while fostering and deepening Iran's connections with Europe, set out forcefully to distinguish Iran from its surrounding Sunni-dominated domain.[5] They transitioned Iran, at times with great brutality, from a mostly Sunni Muslim country into a largely Shi'a state, and successfully defended it against their foremost Sunni rival, the Ottoman Empire (AD 1299–1923), which ruled over most of the largely Sunni Arab world. The Safavids blended Shi'a Islam – a minority sect within the Muslim world (with a majority today only in Iran, Iraq, Bahrain and Azerbaijan) – with the traditional Iranian national heritage to generate a temporal religious foundation for political legitimacy and modern state-building.[6]

However, as in the case of preceding dynasties, internal conflicts, overstretch and poor means of communication rather than foreign aggression resulted in the eventual demise of the Safavids, paving the way for the rise of the Qajar dynasty (AD 1785–1925). The Qajar rulers, who shifted the capital from Shiraz (to where the Safavids had moved their seat of power in the early eighteenth century and near where Cyrus the Great had established the centre of his imperial domain of Persepolis) to Tehran in 1795, eventually found themselves unable to rule their empire effectively. This time, however, the reasons were somewhat different. From the late eighteenth century, the Qajars faced not only growing domestic nationalist and reformist demands from within their realm, but foreign challenges to their authority arising from two rival imperial powers, Tsarist Russia and Great Britain. These two imperial powers competed not only for influence in Iran, but also in the entire region from Istanbul to Tibet in what became known as the 'Great Game'.[7] The later Qajar period was marked largely by the Iranian rulers' efforts to maintain internal order and rebuff foreign encroachment, as Iran fell deeper into the clutches of Anglo-Russian imperial rivalry. This rivalry never led to a direct colonization of Iran, but resulted in a number of other injurious consequences, including substantial territorial losses, the decline of Iranian political autonomy and the diminution of the Qajars' dynastic power and prestige.

Although Iran has for centuries been known as a cultural heartland and political force to be reckoned with, its historical journey was not always smooth or glorious. Successive dictatorial regimes, bouts of severe political repression and civil wars have punctuated and defined Iran's long history since the nation's inception.[8] Iran's modern history has been marked by forced outside impositions and national integration, frequent social unrest and rebellions, ethno-tribal and sectarian conflicts, massive human rights violations and tragic episodes of bloodshed, as well as Iranian aggression against other territorial domains

16

and repulsion of outside forces' transgressions against Iran. Authoritarian political culture and obedience to the ruler and, from the sixteenth century, Twelver Shi'a Islam (whose doctrines were strongly upheld by rulers as a means of heavenly and earthly legitimation), as well as fear of other imperial and imperialist powers, began to take a strong hold on the Iranian people. From that point onwards, the lines between temporal and religious authority were blurred and society became increasingly vulnerable to the changing whims of rulers and internal as well as external exigencies. By the late nineteenth century, the territorial grandeur of Iran's imperial past had vanished, and the country had shrunk more or less to its present size. The Qajar dynasty found itself increasingly preoccupied with serious domestic problems and was constrained by foreign powers.

Oil and politics

In addition to its geostrategic importance, the discovery of oil in Iran at the turn of the twentieth century made the country yet more vulnerable to foreign interference. The discovery was made under a 1901 concession given by Mozzafar al-Din Shah Qajar to a British-born Australian entrepreneur, William Knox D'Arcy, and the concession and corresponding oil resources were thence transferred to the British government within a decade. Having already cajoled Russia, weakened in the wake of the abortive 1905 revolution against the Tsarist rule, into agreeing to a division of Iran into northern and southern spheres of influence in 1907, Britain now also moved to deprive Russia of any access to Iranian oil. British imperial involvement and Russian attempts to rebuff it sparked widespread resentment among the Iranian people, who were proud of their ancient national heritage, enraged at the growing disparity between the privileges of foreigners and the poverty of many Iranians, and determined to preserve their historical independence and identity.[9] The experience of Western imperialism thus fed directly into the rise of Iranian nationalism, which began to oppose the cultural, economic and political domination of Western powers with growing tenacity. Nationalist ideas, imported from the West and combined with homegrown secular and Shi'a Islamic ideologies, gave form and intellectual coherence to many Iranians' desire to reclaim their land for themselves and to repel encroaching foreign influences.

The 1906 constitutional revolution

Together with the Qajar Shah's corrupt and ineffective political system and his failure to engage in progressive structural changes, this set the scene for a crisis of legitimacy and helped to unleash a wave of nationalist movements for reform and freedom from internal repression and outside interference. Leading the movement was a group of Western-inspired intellectuals known as the Constitutionalists, who were supported by small merchant (*bazaari*) and Shi'a clergy (*ulama*) groups.[10] They came from different backgrounds but shared a common goal of transforming Iran from an absolute into a constitutional monarchy and undercutting the traditional Anglo-Russian rivalry in and over Iran. The outcome of their struggle was the Iranian Constitution of 1906, which enshrined, among other things, a significant political role for the *ulama* to oversee the working of the Iranian government in order to make sure that it stayed on the path of Shi'a Islam. The Constitution also provided for the establishment of a parliament (*Majles*), ushering in a quasi-democratic period in Iranian politics. However, the Constitutionalist movement failed to liberalize the Iranian political system or to raise Iran to a position of national and economic independence against the backdrop of an entrenched authoritarian political culture and vested foreign and domestic interests. To make matters worse, Mozaffar al-Din Shah Qajar, the ruler who had been responsible for agreeing to the demands of the Constitutionalist movement, died five days after the signing of the Iranian Constitution.

His successor, Mohammad Ali Shah Qajar, had nothing but contempt for the *Majles* and its supporters. By agreeing to recognize the Anglo-Russian Agreement of 1907, he was able to secure British backing and, in June 1908, to shut down the *Majles,* arresting many of its members and executing a number of leading clerics, provoking national outrage.[11] Mohammad Ali's success in suppressing the Constitutionalists was also helped by the fact that the movement's key participants and leaders shared few common principles beyond their opposition to absolute monarchy and foreign interference: the conservative *ulama* and pro-secular liberals ultimately could not see eye-to-eye on many issues. Thus Iranians remained divided over the future course of their country. While the Constitutionalists were able to depose Mohammad Ali in 1909, instating his 11-year-old son Ahmad as Shah and convening a new *Majles*, Iran's constitutional experiment would reach an end just two years later with a coup, carried out by the boy Shah's regent, with the support of the two major foreign powers.[12] The issues that had prompted

19

the Constitutionalist movement remained unresolved, and this time the Constitutionalists would not recover. At the same time, under the circumstances, the Qajar dynasty was unable to halt its own rapid demise. Iran drifted into deeper social and political chaos, with the British and Soviets occupying part of the Iranian territories between 1918 and 1920.

The rise of the Pahlavis

Against this backdrop, Reza Khan, an illiterate commander who had risen through the ranks of the Russian-trained Cossack Brigade, seized power in a stunning coup in February 1921. In 1925, he assumed the Persian throne and crowned himself as Iran's new Shah. While retaining the *Majles* and the 1906 Constitution as a source of legitimacy, he wore the mantle of his authoritarian predecessors, and established his own dynasty, that of the Pahlavis, which proved to be one of the shortest but most consequential in the long history of Iranian monarchy. Judging by his ideas and deeds, Reza Shah was essentially an autocratic nationalist modernizer, inspired by pro-Western reformist ideas as well as by secularist ideals and achievements of his contemporary Turkish reformer, Mustafa Kemal Ataturk.[13] As would become rapidly apparent, his two main goals were to modernize Iran and reduce British and Russian influence in the country.

To these ends, Reza Shah embarked on a series of socioeconomic reforms aimed at centralizing political power and modernizing Iran economically, militarily and socially. He laid down firm foundations for infrastructural development, the provision of modern social services (education and health in particular) and the strengthening of the security forces, which formed the backbone of his rule. His efforts also included the renegotiation of Britain's oil concessions in 1933, resulting in an ostensibly more favourable arrangement for Iran.[14]

Although intended to create an independent and powerful Iran free from foreign dependence, Reza Shah's reforms were nonetheless politically naive. His modernization initiative along the lines of Westernization outraged a majority of Iranians, most of whom were devout Shi'a Muslims and socially conservative. Furthermore, his attempts to secularize Iran and to curtail the influence of the traditional religious establishment angered the *ulama*. Opposition to the Shah, such as that which erupted in 1935, was met with violent repression and an even faster pace of modernization. Reforms were enforced with brutal resolve, including outlawing the wearing of the headscarf in 1936, which resulted in some women having their veils forcibly removed by policemen on the streets.

The Anglo-Soviet invasion and the rise of Mohammad Reza Pahlavi

Reza Shah, who had displayed considerable admiration for Nazi Germany, which had grown to be Iran's largest trading partner, and Mussolini's Italy, could not ultimately defend Iran and his throne against the British and Soviets. Although rivals in Iran, Britain and the Soviet Union forged an alliance against the common enemy, Germany, and its supporters, in the Second World War. When Reza Shah refused a joint demand by the two powers, backed by the United

21

States, to facilitate the transfer of wartime materiel to the Soviet Union through his country, Anglo-Russian forces responded by jointly occupying Iran in 1941, along almost the same lines according to which they had divided the country into their respective spheres of influence under the infamous 1907 St Petersburg Agreement. The Soviets thus took over the five northern provinces, the British occupied the southern provinces, where the oil fields were located, and Tehran's government was left in control of a middle strip to symbolize the country's sovereignty and independence.

Meanwhile, the Allied powers agreed to end their occupation of Iran within six months after the termination of war. Reza Shah was forced to abdicate and went into exile in Johannesburg, where he died in 1944 as a frustrated nationalist and modernizer. In his stead the Allied forces appointed his eldest son, Mohammad Reza, to mount the Peacock Throne. Mohammad Reza Shah Pahlavi, who was 21, inexperienced and vulnerable to manipulation, wielded very little power during the early years of his reign, and could do little but stand by and witness the resurgence of Anglo-Soviet rivalry in his divided country, despite the two powers' newly forged cooperation at the international level.[15]

The oil nationalization crisis and the 1953 coup

As humiliating as it was, the Allied occupation resulted in two important developments that would prove significant for the subsequent trajectory of Iran's history. The first was that it saw the emergence of a new convergence of interest between American forces, British forces, the Shah and the latter's conservative supporters, which came together in a common effort to repel

Soviet and internal communist influence after the war. This development became more important with the onset of the Cold War and the consequent emergence of the US–Soviet superpower rivalry in the Middle East. Given its geostrategic vitality as an immediate neighbour of the Soviet Union and its tremendous energy reserves, Iran quickly became a very valuable prize for the West and an even more critical one to retain in the effort to prevent the spread of Soviet communism.

The second important development was that under the Allied occupation, the centralized political control that Reza Shah had built loosened considerably. This resulted in a weakening of the state and a strengthening of society, which had hitherto been suppressed. The outcome was the ascent of various political and social groups with reformist agendas, which, like the supporters of the Constitutionalist movement, held a wide range of ideological platforms and perspectives. Some of these, such as the pro-Soviet communist *Tudeh* (Masses) Party and the conservative *Erade-ye Melli*, were backed by international powers (the Soviets and British respectively). Others developed in the vein of Iranian nationalism and opposition to foreign encroachment and monopoly of Iranian resources.

The National Front (*Jebhe-ye Melli*), which from 1949 began to emerge as a strongly consolidated rainbow nationalist movement, was one such group. At its head was the veteran nationalist and seasoned politician, Mohammad Mossadeq.[16] He had served as a member of parliament during the Constitutionalist period, had opposed Reza Shah's assumption of the throne on the grounds that it would produce another dictatorship, and had subsequently been jailed for his opposition activities in 1940. Mossadeq had all along pushed for a revolutionary process of change that

23

would transform Iran into a constitutional monarchy, nationalize Iran's oil industry and use Iran's oil income to implement overdue social and economic reforms to ameliorate living conditions for the majority of the Iranian public. He was deeply troubled by the costs that the Anglo-Russian rivalry had inflicted upon Iranians and Iran, and was keen to see its quick demise.[17]

The British and Soviet forces withdrew from Iran after the Second World War as had been agreed, although the Soviets did so very reluctantly. They had nonetheless turned Iran into an arena of intense rivalry, marking the earliest phase of the Cold War that took off from the late 1940s. With Mossadeq's popularity soaring due to his principled and committed leadership, the National Front gained a majority in the *Majles*. In April 1951, the National Front-dominated *Majles* nominated Mossadeq to the position of prime minister, leaving the Shah with no choice but to act constitutionally and appoint him to that position on 30 April 1951. The next day Mossadeq nationalized the Anglo-Iranian Oil Company (AIOC), which the British had founded to control Iranian oil resources. He did so not only to maximize Iran's income from and ownership of its oil industry for its own benefit, but also to minimize the reasons for the British and Soviets to continue their rivalry in Iran, as the British hold on the Iranian oil industry had constantly impelled the Soviets to make demands for a similar share. Mossadeq also implemented a number of measures to constitutionally limit the powers of the monarchy, to advance structural political, social and economic reforms, and to pursue a policy of neutrality in world politics.

This was not only enough to alienate the Shah and his conservative supporters, who had developed close links with the British and the Americans, but also to incur the wrath of the British, who reacted by sending the Royal Navy to impose an embargo on Iranian oil exports. Although the United States had initially backed Mossadeq's nationalization as part of a subtle policy of driving the British out of the Middle East to enable American oil companies to secure a share in Iranian oil resources, Washington was ultimately persuaded by the British that the Mossadeq government was going to fall and that a likely alternative to it would be a Soviet-backed communist government, led by the *Tudeh* Party. From mid-1952, fearing the loss of an oil-rich frontline state to the Soviet Union in the Cold War, the United States began to align itself with the British over the situation in Iran.[18]

By late 1952, the British embargo was beginning to have the desired economic and political effect of damaging Mossadeq's popularity and undermining his coalition. At the same time, in a dramatic turn of events, the Shah (who found himself increasingly side-lined by Mossadeq's attempts to curtail the power of the monarchy) left Iran for Switzerland in August 1953. Convinced that this was part of a Soviet-orchestrated plot against the Shah's pro-Western monarchy, the Central Intelligence Agency (CIA), backed by the British MI6, engineered a coup against the elected, reformist government of Mossadeq, and within a week brought a somewhat reluctant Shah back to Iran to reassume his throne.[19] From this point on, the Shah would govern Iran at the behest of the United States. Mossadeq, for his part, was put under house arrest until his death in 1967. The Shah and his supporters imposed a military dictatorship, maintained through severe political repression and extensive use of the brutal secret police, the Organization of National Information and Security (*Sazeman-e Ettela'at va Amniyat-e Keshvar*) or what became known as SAVAK, which was set up by the CIA and the Federal Bureau of Investigation (FBI) in cooperation with Israel's intelligence service, Mossad.[20] Over the course of the next two decades, SAVAK would become notorious through its role in maintaining the Shah's autocratic rule, at the cost of hundreds if not thousands of Iranian lives.

Iran in the US orbit, 1953–79

The United States provided massive financial, economic and military assistance, and signed various bilateral agreements with Iran to shore up the Shah's regime. The US–Iranian relationship rapidly transitioned into one of 'patron–client', underpinned by enduring structures of Iran's dependence on and vulnerability to Washington. Iran was speedily transformed into a frontline bulwark against Soviet communism, with the consequence that the country lost the neutrality in world politics that Mossadeq had cherished and that Reza Shah had carefully managed. The Shah publicly identified the Soviet threat as a key concern for his government and Iran, and therefore rationalized his alliance with the United States as a necessity. He highlighted the ideals and values that Iran and America held in common, and joined the US-backed, British-orchestrated regional Baghdad Pact (with its other members being Pakistan, Iraq and Turkey) in 1955 and its successor, the Central Treaty Organization (CENTO), three years later after a successful Arab nationalist coup in Iraq and the withdrawal of that country from the Pact. All this underscored Iran's drift into the US camp in opposition to the Soviet Union. While sharing Mossadeq's idea of Iran's ownership and control of its oil resources for the benefit of the Iranian people, the Shah criticized the former prime minister for pursuing his objectives through a policy of 'negative nationalism' as opposed to what he called 'positive nationalism'.[21]

Meanwhile, the United States became the deciding actor in resolving the Anglo-Iranian oil nationalization dispute. It proposed and set up an international consortium, called the Iranian Oil Participants Ltd, which became operational from late 1954, to run the Iranian oil industry. In the process, it ended the British monopoly of Iranian oil resources by enabling five American oil companies, which had been lobbying for a substantial stake in Iranian oil resources since the early 1940s, to have shares equal to those of British Petroleum in the consortium.

Following his empowerment by the CIA-orchestrated coup and the sidelining of major opposition, the Shah pursued two contradictory goals that would ultimately lead to his overthrow in the revolution of 1978/79. The first was to make himself pivotal and indispensable to the operation of Iranian governance through a process of political centralization. This tactic had been critical for the survival of Persian monarchies for centuries, but was at odds with the ideas of constitutional monarchy that took root in Iran at the beginning of the twentieth century. The second was to engage in a secular, capitalist mode of national social and economic development and foreign policy behaviour that would complement his special relationship with the United States. However, by the late 1950s, both Washington and the Shah had come to the conclusion that it would be necessary for the Iranian monarchy to widen its support base if its long-term survival and uncritical US backing were to be ensured. The Shah thus put a formal end

rtial law in 1959. Subsequently, under pressure
... the John F. Kennedy administration, he intensified efforts to secure a wider base of popular legitimacy
by inaugurating a reform programme in what he called
the 'White Revolution' or the 'Revolution of the Shah
and People'.[22]

However, whatever steps he took to embed himself
at the centre of Iranian politics and popularize his
regime, the Shah could never expunge the indignity of
being reinstalled on the throne by the CIA, bridge the
contradiction in his goals, or transform his relationship
with the United States into one of interdependence in
order to elevate his rule in the eyes of most Iranians as
well as the countries of the region, which viewed him
as an 'American puppet'. He continued to rule by suppression, cooptation, patronage and divide-and-rule
politics. He projected an image of SAVAK as all-
powerful and ever-present, to the extent that 'people
could not trust people'.[23] All forms of opposition were
outlawed as the Shah set out forcefully to demolish
any other potential or actual centres of power that
could possibly challenge his authority. This included
the Shi'a religious establishment, which remained very
influential with a majority of the Iranian people, especially in the urban slums and rural areas. The Shah
sought to limit or coopt the influence of the Shi'a
clerics (*ulama*) through such measures as seizing their
religious endowments (*waqf*), closing their schools and
harassing, imprisoning and exiling the defiant ones. He
wanted now to be respected not only in the manner of
Iran's ancient emperors, but also to be equated with
Ali ibn Musa al-Rida (AD 765–819), commonly known
as Imam Reza, after whom he claimed to have been
named. According to Shi'a beliefs, Imam Reza was the
eighth of the Twelve Shi'a Imams, with the twelfth and

last being Imam Muhammad ibn Hassan al-Mahdi, who disappeared in the tenth century, to reappear prior to the Day of Judgement. While many Iranians felt humiliated and remained deeply distressed about what was happening to them and their country, the Shah's rule continued. With the help of almost unqualified US support and increased oil revenue deriving from the collective bargaining power of the Organization of the Petroleum Exporting Countries (OPEC), founded in 1960 and becoming particularly lucrative from the early 1970s, the Shah continued not only to hold onto power; he also increasingly indulged in luxurious displays of wealth while implementing policies in pursuit of visions of Iranian imperial grandeur. In 1967, he held an official coronation ceremony where he elevated himself to the title of Mohammad Reza Shah Pahlavi Shahanshah Aryamehr (King of Kings and Light of the Aryans). The explosion of Iran's oil revenues from US$1 billion in 1970 to close to US$20 billion in 1974 – a development in which the Shah played a leading, positive role through OPEC – and favourable changes in the regional and global situation meant that the Shah finally had an opportunity to put Iran's relations with the United States on a somewhat symmetrical basis.

The flood of oil revenue led the Shah to become more grandiose in his ambitions for himself and Iran. He decided that he would move Iran 'Towards the Great Civilization' (Be Suye Tamadon-e Bozorg), an idea that he discussed in his book published under the same title in 1977.[24] In doing so, he believed that he would transform Iran not only into the regional superpower, but also into the world's fifth largest economic and military power by the mid-1980s. He drew on the main resource he had at his disposal – Iranian

29

petro-dollar capital – to pursue his dreams of elevating Iran to regional and global leadership on a model he imagined stretched back to Cyrus the Great and his imperial successors. Otherwise, he and Iran had little in the way of non-capital goods, know-how, trained manpower or infrastructural capacity to achieve the Shah's grandiose designs within such a short period.

In pursuit of these opulent ambitions, the Shah embarked on an equally poorly conceived and badly implemented import-based programme of economic, social and military modernization, which was neither responsive nor suitable to conditions within Iran. By 1977, as part of this programme, the Shah had the largest navy in the Persian Gulf, the most modern air force in the region and the fifth largest military force in the world.[25] The cost of this, however, was that economic development lagged behind military build-up, and social development – including education and health – lagged further behind the other two. As the backbone of the Shah's rule and vision, military and security modernization were given priority over social and economic change. The programme caused tremendous social and economic disparities, bottlenecks and dislocation (including massive migration from the countryside to urban centres, resulting in urban congestion and ghettoization, as well as a decline in agricultural production), uncertainty and increasing popular disillusionment. As a result, the Shah's so-called 'White Revolution' and 'Towards the Great Civilization' projects quickly proved unviable.[26]

Meanwhile, the Shah's military build-up was beginning to alarm Iran's Arab neighbours. From 1972, the United States provided the Shah with a *carte blanche* for whatever weapons systems he wanted to buy, short of nuclear ones, as a way of not only building a

powerful ally under the 'Nixon Doctrine', but also recy-
cling the money that Western countries were paying for
higher Iranian oil prices back into US coffers. Given the
historical, cultural, sectarian and political differences
between historically Shi'a Iran and its predominantly
Sunni Arab neighbours (with the exception of the
Shi'a majority but Sunni minority-ruled Iraq), the
latter – most of them oil-rich – could not be expected
to share the United States' enthusiasm for the Shah's
military build-up, which they sought to counter in two
ways. One was to engage in similar build-ups, and
the other was to act within OPEC to keep oil prices
down, with Saudi Arabia – the largest producer within
OPEC – playing a leading role in the process. The first
development resulted in a regional arms race, and the
second seriously squeezed Iran's oil income, prompt-
ing the Shah by 1975 to look for loans in Europe in
order to fund his modernization programmes on the
one hand, and to take steps to dampen Iranian people's
rising expectations on the other.

The main beneficiary of the dramatic hike in weapons
purchases was the United States and, to a considerable
extent, Britain, France and Germany, which also sold
arms to Iran. The weapons bought by the Shah and,
for that matter, by its Arab neighbours, could only be
used in regional interstate conflicts and not against the
Soviet Union – a reality that would tragically prove to
be the case in the subsequent eight-year war between
Iran and Iraq (1980–88). The oil-for-weapons arrangements that became the norm for Middle Eastern
countries during this period contributed significantly to
the increase in volatility and violence within the region
over the course of the next few decades.

Despite the stirrings and signs of trouble in the mid-
1970s, the Shah continued to feel tall, and the United

States was proud to have a strong and reliable ally to help it contain the Soviet Union, and maintain and strengthen its superpower dominance in the oil-rich but volatile Middle East. Although the Western oil companies after 1973 were no longer in control of the oil resources or pricing of the commodity in the region, as OPEC had wrested both of these for its member states, they still remained in full control of marketing Middle Eastern oil at record profits and acting in concert with their governments. However, the Shah's rule and US-led Western support of him and his regime was widely resented within Iran and criticized in the region. Many Iranian people longed for the day when they could see their nation rise to fulfil Ferdowsi's and Nezami's words, and become the 'heart of the world' once again.

Origins of the 1979 revolution

By the late 1960s, four major sources of opposition to the Shah's rule had emerged in Iran. The first came from ideological and political organizations, including various Marxist and nationalist groups. The most radical of these groups ranged from *Mujahideen-e Khalq* (Warriors for the People), which preached a mixture of Marxism and Islamism, to the militant Maoist *Feda'iyan-e Khalq* (Sacrificers for People), to the pro-Soviet *Tudeh* Party, and to some extent Mossadeq's former party, the centre-left nationalist *Jebhe-ye Melli*. The first two of these groups had, by the turn of the 1970s, commenced a series of violent operations targeting government officials and American personnel. The second source of opposition comprised pro-democracy reformists, who were generally drawn from the upper stratum of Iranian society, and included various ad hoc networks of intellectuals, professionals and civil servants. The third included merchants and petit bourgeois (*bazaaris*) who could no longer benefit from the Shah's economic and taxation policies and who found his pro-Western policies undesirable in light of their more traditional lifestyles and values. The fourth came from the Shi'a religious establishment, which increasingly found the Shah's secular politics, dictatorial infringement upon their historically safeguarded domain and perceived subordination to the United States to be repugnant. The Shi'a religious establishment felt alienated from its self-assumed constitutional responsibility of ensuring the conformity of the government to Shi'a Islamic precepts. By the late 1970s, public grievances had also gathered pace among different levels of society that had been adversely affected by the Shah's ill-conceived programme of reform and widespread corruption. A deepening rift between two ways of life – one traditional, and one modern and Western – was becoming increasingly obvious.

Of all those disaffected by the Shah's regime, the group that managed to remain relatively cohesive by the late 1970s were the Shi'a *ulama*. An important reason for this was that the Shah was anxious not to appear sacrilegious in his attempts to erode the traditional power of the Shi'a establishment. As a result, the mosque had remained the one place that SAVAK could not easily infiltrate and invade. The network of mosques had provided sanctuary and a safe forum for clerical critics of the Shah.

Prominent among the disconcerted clerics, but by no means the most senior or well-known Iranian religious figure at the time, was Ayatollah Ruhollah

Khomeini.[27] He came from a learned religious family and was educated in Shi'a Islamic studies in the city of Qom, a traditional seat of Shi'a learning and source of Shi'a political and social influence in Iran. Khomeini had emerged as a strong religious critic of what he regarded as the Shah's policies of 'capitulation' to the United States as early as 1961, when he supported the teachers' strike for better pay and working conditions. Within three years, these activities would lead to his imprisonment and then exile in Turkey and Iraq.

Although more junior than other clerics in the Shi'ite religious hierarchy, such as Grand Ayatollah Mohammad Kazem Shariatmadari and Ayatollah Hossein-Ali Montazeri, Khomeini's assessment of Iran's political situation nevertheless found a wide audience in the tumultuous climate of the 1970s. Disseminated illegally in the form of pamphlets and cassette tapes, Khomeini's message presented Iran's situation in radical, religiously charged terms. He dichotomized the world between the realm of *mostakbarin* (the oppressors) and *mosta'zafin* (the downtrodden and oppressed), and called for the latter's empowerment – by force where necessary. In Iraq (1965–79) he found sanctuary among the country's majority Shi'a population and was permitted by the Iraqi dictator, Saddam Hussein, to engage in anti-Shah activities due to adversarial relations between the two leaders. From exile, Khomeini electrified young clerics by calling on them to abandon their traditional contentment with overseeing the work of government in favour of seizing the reins of power themselves. Through his tapes, which were smuggled into Iran and played in sermons during Friday prayers in the mosques, Khomeini managed to build a wide network of clerical and non-clerical supporters. In contrast to the elaborate ideologies of many of the Shah's political opponents, Khomeini's Islamic message was simple and accessible, and resonated deeply with a majority of Iranians who had been imbued with Shi'a Islamic religious culture over the centuries.[28]

Revolution and the return of Khomeini

Pushed by the Jimmy Carter administration's foreign policy emphasis on human rights, the Shah found it expedient from the mid-1970s to commence a policy of gradual and limited liberalization, intended to mollify the opposition. Instead, the situation snowballed from a wave of protests in October 1977 into a nationwide uprising, and ultimately a popular revolution.[29] While the participants were drawn from diverse social strata, the Shah's suppression of all forms of organized political opposition and his 1975 institution of a single-party system under *Rastakhiz* ('Resurgence' Party) meant that Khomeini's religious message and mosque network – which remained beyond the reach of SAVAK – proved increasingly influential. In 1977, Khomeini's supporters within the Shi'a establishment had formed the anti-Shah Society of Combatant Clerics (*Jame'eh-ye Ruhaniyat-e Mobarez*). The protests were initially spearheaded by a rainbow movement of the Shah's political and professional opponents in pursuit of constitutional and democratic reforms. However, since the movement was made up of diverse groups and individuals, with no common platform beyond opposition to the Shah's regime, Khomeini and his supporters, as the most organized, disciplined and dedicated cluster, were able by the second half of 1978 to seize the leadership of the revolution.

35

From September, Khomeini emerged as the most prominent figure among the *ulama* to whom leaders of other groups deferred in the expectation that this would not undermine their chances of achieving their main objective of systemic reform. At first, Khomeini appeared to be nuanced and conciliatory in his approach. But as his popularity and grip on the movement grew, and as the Shah failed in his crackdown and resorted to making one concession after another to the opposition, Khomeini revealed that he would not be a man of compromise. For him, there was only one ideology and direction, and that was his Islamic one. He would settle for nothing less than the abdication of the Shah. The Shah was finally forced to hand over power to one of his political opponents, the deputy leader of the National Front, Shapur Bakhtiar, before leaving Tehran on 17 January 1979 for a 'temporary stay' abroad. The circumstances of the Shah's departure were strikingly similar to those of his father nearly 40 years earlier, and, like the latter, his temporary stay abroad would become a permanent exile. The new Prime Minister Bakhtiar could neither stem the popular tide calling for Khomeini's return nor prevent the already weakened structures of the Shah's control from crumbling. Two weeks after the Shah's departure, Khomeini returned to Tehran from exile in Paris, where Saddam Hussein had banished him six months earlier under pressure from the Shah's government. He received a tumultuous welcome from millions of Iranians, although most of them knew very little about him beyond his determined opposition to the Shah's regime and its foreign backers.

As for the Shah, he became a refugee moving from one place to another in the West. Even his staunch ally, the United States, now refused to support him. Tehran clamoured for the Shah to stand trial for crimes against the Iranian people and warned Washington of retaliation should it shelter the Shah. Nonetheless, after much lobbying by the Shah's old friend and former US Secretary of State Henry Kissinger, the Carter administration finally allowed the Shah to be admitted to hospital in New York for treatment of advanced lymphatic cancer on 22 October 1979. Although this allowed him a short respite, he was prompted to leave the United States quickly, and the whole episode only further angered Khomeini and his supporters. Later, in a dash of mercy, Egyptian President Anwar al-Sadat invited the Shah to reside in Cairo, where he died at the age of 61 on 27 July 1980.

The Iranian revolution, which was a larger mass uprising than any revolution before it, took most by surprise. Khomeini and his supporters had certainly not anticipated it. The United States, as the main foreign power in Iran, with plenty of intelligence on the ground, did not foresee it. As late as October 1977, President Carter was still publicly praising the Shah as the United States' most cherished and stable ally. It was not until 8 December 1978 that he finally cast doubt on the survival of the Shah's reign – something which may have emboldened the Shah's opponents and expedited his downfall.[30] Not even the seasoned American Middle East hands, in which the US government and academic institutions had heavily invested, could see the clouds gathering in preparation for an extraordinary storm in Iran. The success of the Iranian revolution opened a new and unlooked-for chapter in Iran's evolution from a traditionalist monarchy to an Islamic republic under the supreme religious and political leadership of Ayatollah Khomeini.

3

The Islamic Order

Those who came together to overthrow the Shah in the 1978/79 Iranian revolution did so for very different reasons and with very different visions of Iran's future direction. Many wanted a democratic Iran, some aimed at a socialist Iran, and others desired an Islamic Iran within conflicting approaches and frameworks. Until the Shah's downfall, the factor that had united them was simply their opposition to his rule. Once the Shah had gone, the movement had little in common, in either ideological or aspirational terms, to keep it together. The result was a scramble for power in pursuit of what direction a post-Shah Iran should take. However, in a matter of weeks the question of who would lead Iran, and in which direction, was resolved. After his return from exile on 1 February 1979, Ayatollah Ruhollah Khomeini would consolidate his personal hold on power as religious and political leader extraordinaire. On 1 April 1979, less than two months after his jubilant reception in Tehran, he would declare Iran an Islamic Republic and thereby reveal his unshakeable goal: the creation of an Islamic polity, in strict accordance with Khomeini's own definition of that concept. The Islamic order that emerged out of these developments was both highly complex and, in its early phases, uncompromising towards internal and external opposition. What was the nature of this order? What conditions drove its establishment and development? How has it been sustained, to what extent has it proved functional, and to what extent can we expect it to remain so in the future? In addressing these questions, one needs to analyse the intellectual and institutional origins of the Islamic Republic and, in doing so, to shed light on which factors came to make the Iranian system unique as well as a source of major discomfort for many, especially in the West, and specifically in the United States.

From an Iranian to an Islamic revolution

In the early stages of the revolution, when the role of the clerical opposition was still highly limited, Khomeini was careful not to say too much about his specific ambitions for Iran's future. As such, he declined to clarify whether he would seek to transform what had started as an anti-Shah revolution into an Islamic one in order to change Iran into an Islamic state, defined by a Shi'a religious order. He seems to have purposefully cultivated an image of himself as politically inclusive. As early as 1970, Khomeini had touted the theory of an 'Islamic government' or *velayat-e faqih* (Guardianship of the Jurist) in a published version of several of his speeches from exile in Najaf, Iraq. At no point in these speeches, however, did he elaborate on how actionable his theory would be.[1] It was not until the later months of the revolution, when leadership was within his grasp and he was convinced that the Shah's days were numbered, that Khomeini opted to voice a clearer articulation of his understanding of Islamic government

39

and how it should be brought about. In an interview with the French newspaper *Le Monde* on 17 October 1978, when asked what he meant by an 'Islamic government', he replied: 'We do not intend to take over the government. But the religious leaders direct the people in order to define the goals and the demands of Islam. Since the majority of the Iranian people are Muslim, an Islamic government also means that it is a government supported by the majority.' He further asserted that the Islamic government would be established in stages: 'the first stage [will entail expelling] all the exploiters and colonizers whoever they may be' and deploying Iran's resources for the benefit of the Iranian people; 'the second stage will see the complete purging of [all] the traitors [and] the corrupt ... [and then] other stages would follow' – but as for what these might be, he did not elaborate.[2]

It is important to note that Khomeini was not the first Iranian ayatollah with political ambitions. There had been several before him since the turn of the century. One of his most prominent and influential predecessors was Ayatollah Abol-Ghasen Kashani (1882–1962), who served as Chairman of the *Majles* during Mohammad Mossadeq's premiership and played a key role in the events of the oil nationalization crisis. Known for his advocacy of an Islamic government, 'with a stance against oppression, despotism, colonialism and excessive capitalism', Kashani initially made common cause with political secularist Mossadeq in backing his oil nationalization, but subsequently, when Mossadeq refused to give Kashani's supporters a meaningful share in the executive power, he turned against the premier, which precipitated his downfall.[3]

Khomeini, like most inside and outside of Iran, had not initially foreseen the coming of the revolution and the fall of the Shah, nor the speed and the manner in which these would occur. Up to the point of his return, he had only loosely visualized what an Iranian Islamic state should be like. Beyond this, he had not voiced a clear strategy for implementing his vision until the latest stages of the revolution. Nor did he and his close companions and devotees have the necessary policy or administrative experience to handle an Islamic transformation of an Iran that had been subject to intensive secularization under the Shah and which was closely linked to the United States and the international capitalist market system. A further complicating issue was that by the time Khomeini assumed stewardship of Iran, most of the country's state apparatus had virtually collapsed, and what was left was rapidly subjected to purging and dismantling. This generated a power vacuum that various groups, with different ideological and political dispositions, vied to fill. It was only after Khomeini was catapulted to power that it became very clear that he and his cohort wanted no less than a wholesale transformation of Iran into Khomeini's vision of a Shi'a Islamic polity, involving, in particular, opposition to the US and Israel.

The key political clerics who surrounded Khomeini now included the shrewd strategic tactician and political organizer, Ayatollah Mohammad Beheshti, who was Khomeini's first designated heir, but who was killed in a bomb blast engineered by Khomeini's political opponents in June 1981; Hashemi Rafsanjani, one of Khomeini's most trusted confidantes, who headed the *Majles* and was later elected as president for two terms (1989–97); Ali Khamenei, who served as president from 1981 to 1989 and succeeded Khomeini as Supreme Leader after his death in July 1989; and Mohammad Reza Mahdavi Kani, a hardline cleric who

41

served the Islamic government from the beginning in prominent positions and who remained an influential player on the Iranian political scene until his death in October 2014.

Among the most prominent non-clerical advisers to Khomeini was the French-educated son of an ayatollah, Seyyad Abol-Hassan Bani-Sadr. He had closely accompanied Khomeini when the latter was in exile in Paris, and he was elected as Iran's first Islamic president in February 1980, only to be forced out of office and into exile in Paris 16 months later, events in which Beheshti played an important role. A second important non-clerical figure in Khomeini's circle was the mild-mannered and liberal-minded Mehdi Bazargan, who served as prime minister for nearly a year in 1979. Although it is not easy to quantify the input that these figures may have had in shaping the system of Islamic governance that was instituted in the next few years, what remains beyond question is that Khomeini's guidance and dictates stood supreme and ultimately prevailed along every step of the way.

Khomeini commenced the process of Islamization of state and society with a national referendum on 30–31 March 1979, which simply asked the people whether they wanted to replace the monarchy with an Islamic Republic. Although the public had not been appraised of what was meant by an Islamic Republic and what it involved, the result of the referendum, in which 97 per cent of voters voiced support for an Islamic state, provided Khomeini with a clear mandate to declare the revolution Islamic and to transform Iran into an Islamic Republic.

Several factors explain why Khomeini was able to establish himself as the supreme authority in the nation and to implement his vision of an Islamic state.

The first was his prominence within the Society of Combative Clerics (*Jame'eh-ye Ruhaniyat-e Mobarez*, or SAC), which had been set up prior to the start of the revolution, with the goal of establishing an Islamic political order in Iran. SAC did not represent the whole of the Iranian Shi'a establishment, but its founders included most of Iran's future political Islamic leaders, notably Khamenei, Rafsanjani and Mahdavi Kani, all of whom had been taught by Khomeini. By the second half of 1978, SAC was able to assume the leadership of the revolutionary movement, dramatically expanding Khomeini's influence in Iran.

Second, although he lacked the clerical seniority of many of his fellow ayatollahs, Khomeini possessed a greater popular ideological appeal than any of them. Moreover, in contrast to the elaborate and secularist ideologies of many of the Shah's political opponents, Khomeini's radically simplified Islamic message resonated with many Iranians. His dichotomization of the world between the oppressors and the downtrodden, and his championing of the latter's cause, found widespread support. His call for the political primacy of the *ulama* (the learned scholars of Islam) galvanized a generation of young clerics.

Third, neither the other Shi'ite clerics nor the secular parties could produce any leader capable of competing with Khomeini's personal charisma and aura, which derived in part from his enigmatic status: the public knew enough about his opposition to the Shah's regime and his clerical modesty and honesty to respect him, but not enough to make a critical assessment of him. Finally, Khomeini's own abilities played a role, as he possessed sufficient political astuteness to meld these advantages with the tide of popular emotion that gripped Iran by 1979.

Khomeini's vision

As mentioned earlier, Khomeini had theorized the idea of an Islamic government for some time,[4] starting with a series of lectures (19 in total) in Iraq, which were later printed and disseminated within Iran and outside the country under the title of *Velayat-e Faqih*. In his lectures, Khomeini denounced monarchy as antithetical to Islam and called for the establishment of an Islamic political order centred on the principle of *velayat-e faqih*.[5] While asserting that all political sovereignty belonged ultimately to God, he defended the concept of *velayat-e faqih* as necessary for the implementation of God's laws within the state. Political power was to be entrusted to a learned jurist (*faqih*), whose unparalleled expertise in Islamic jurisprudence (*fiqh*) and law (*shari'a*) made him uniquely qualified for this task.[6]

Khomeini's political theory also incorporated a notion of popular legitimacy; thus, while Iran would have a Twelver Shi'a political order, this order would at the same time be pluralistic and participatory within an Islamic framework. Khomeini therefore envisioned the Islamic Republic in terms of a constructive interplay in which the divine would enforce the popular and the popular would uphold the divine, creating a two-tier theocratic/pluralistic system of governance that would establish justice, particularly through the empowerment of the downtrodden, within the Iranian state.

The Islamic Republic

Although in the past he had insisted that he would 'not become a president nor accept any other leadership role',[7] Khomeini set out to vigorously enforce a

44

political order in which the divinely ordained position of Supreme Leader (*vali-e faqih*) would provide overarching and determining guidance, while the government beneath it would embody the will of the people within an Islamic frame. This two-tiered system of governance was formalized by the country's Islamic Constitution, which was adopted by another referendum in October 1979.[8] The Constitution upheld both the 'sovereignty of God', embodied in the position of a *vali-e faqih*, and provided for the 'sovereignty of the people' to represent the will of the people through participation and contestation in the political system, ensuring that Islamic governance also rested on a pillar of popular legitimacy. To give expression to this second tier, the Constitution prescribed an elected presidential system of government composed of executive, legislative and judicial branches that reflected Khomeini's understanding of the relationship between popular and divine sovereignty.

As the Islamic order took shape, it showed itself to be highly complex and prone to fragmentation, conflict and manipulation by various forces. Whereas the 'sovereignty of God' was to be established through the position of the Supreme Leader, the sovereignty of the people was to materialize through a government composed of an elected president, a unicameral National Assembly (*Majles*) and an appointed judiciary. The prominence of the presidential system and National Assembly, however, was to be counterbalanced by three other powerful bodies that mediated between the position of the Supreme Leader and the government.

One was the unelected 12-member Council of Guardians (*Shora-ye Negahban-e Qanun-e Asasi*), made up of six experts in Islamic law nominated by the Supreme Leader and six jurists nominated by the head

45

of the judiciary (himself nominated by the Supreme Leader). The Council was entrusted with the power to vet presidential and parliamentary candidates, hold referenda, veto legislation passed in the *Majles* and declare the results of elections. The second was the 86-member Assembly of Experts (*Majles-e Khebregan-e Rahbari*), whose members were to be elected, subject to vetting by the Council of Guardians. This body was tasked with appointing the Supreme Leader, ensuring his adherence to the precepts of Shi'a Islam and terminating his appointment if necessary. The third was the Expediency Council (*Majma'e Tashkhis-e Maslahat-e Nezam*), an administrative assembly appointed by the Supreme Leader with the power to adjudicate legislative disputes between the National Assembly and the Council of Guardians.

Beyond this, various legal, political and security structures and law enforcement agencies, as well as institutional checks and balances, were created. However, the constraints and power-sharing arrangements within the Iranian government were not intended to curtail the power of the Supreme Leader himself, who was invested with ultimate divine and constitutional authority over the executive branch as well as national policy. The governing apparatus was rapidly complemented with the establishment of various extra-political revolutionary and rule-enforcing organizations, composed of cadres who were completely dependent on Khomeini's patronage and that of his senior clerical followers, who were totally devoted to enforcing Khomeini's vision.

From the beginning, Khomeini's leadership and immense popularity ensured that no one could surpass him as the natural choice for the all-powerful position of *vali-e faqih*, to which he was immediately, unquestioningly and constitutionally elevated. This not only put him at the zenith of spiritual and political power in the land, but also reconfirmed him as a *marja'e taqlid* (source of emulation) – the highest rank within the Iranian Shi'a establishment. Khomeini's supporters had already begun to revere him as an 'Imam' during the revolution, a title traditionally reserved in Twelver Shi'a Islam for the descendants of Ali ibn Talib (AD 599–661). Ali was the fourth Caliph (successor to Prophet Mohammad's leadership) and is upheld by Shi'as as the only legitimate successor of the Prophet's leadership and therefore as their first Imam.[9] Following his enthronement as Supreme Leader, Khomeini's authority was sanctified to the extent that any criticism of him or political dissidence came to be seen by his devotees as tantamount to blasphemy and treason. Little or no distinction was made between some of the clerical and non-clerical critics of Khomeini in this respect; any and all individuals who appeared to challenge Khomeini's authority became equally vulnerable to suspicion and persecution. These included some senior figures from the ranks of those who had actively supported the revolution and had been closely associated with Khomeini, but were now either in variance with his vision or were suspected of disloyalty, an issue to which we will return later.

The Islamic Republic under Khomeini, 1979–89

Despite the triumph of the referendum and its aftermath, Khomeini and his supporters still could not expect smooth sailing in their path to establishing an Islamic Republic. As noted previously, there were other forces that had also played a critical role in the revolution, many of which held divergent ideological dispositions and different aspirations for Iran's post-Shah transformation. Although the Islamic Constitution was quickly endorsed and adopted, domestic opposition remained a potentially serious problem for the government. In addition to his clerical critics, Khomeini was confronted by the hostility of many secular or semi-secular organizations that had deferred to his authority in the final stages of the revolution, but could not be supportive of his vision of an Islamic state. These were mostly radical leftist organizations, such as the *Mujahideen-e Khalq*, *Feda'iyan-e Khalq* and *Tudeh*, but also included the centre-left nationalist *Jebhe-ye Melli*. Although these groups lacked a common platform and would become increasingly splintered in the aftermath of the revolution, their willingness to engage in violence for political ends made them a serious threat to the embryonic Islamic Republic.

Faced with this precarious situation, Khomeini opted for a two-dimensional approach to implementing his Islamic vision: *jihadi* and *ijtihadi*.[10] Although each term has a complex history in Islamic thought, *jihadi* may be taken here to signify a combative, revolutionary and inward-looking approach to the implementation of Islam; *ijtihadi*, on the other hand, denotes a reformist and creative interpretation and application of Islam, based on independent human reasoning. While many have come to identify Khomeini with the first approach, it is important to note that he was renowned among Shi'a clerics for his *ijtihadi* tendencies and that many of the ideas he advanced – such as *velayat-e faqih* – have been seen as innovative and unorthodox. Some Iranian *ulama* have even gone so far as to view some of Khomeini's rulings as *bida'a*, or illegitimate innovation, according to Islam.[11]

Nevertheless, it was Khomeini's *jihadi* approach to Iran's transformation that characterized the early years of the Islamic Republic. He pursued this approach against the backdrop of, and in many ways in lock step with, Iran's centuries-old authoritarian political culture. In this period, as opposition mounted, with such groups as the *Mujahideen-e Khalq* and *Feda'iyan-e Khalq* resorting to violence, Khomeini's supporters moved forcefully, often acting extra-judicially and brutally, to achieve three *jihadi* objectives.

The first was, as Khomeini had foreshadowed in the latter part of the revolution, the elimination of all domestic resistance and opposition. This included both those who had participated in the Shah's regime or had closely sympathized with it, and many who had opposed the Shah, but stood against the Islamic Republic. The early years of the revolution were marked by violent turmoil in which between 10,000 and 20,000 Iranians, who were denounced as 'oppressors' (*mostakbarin*) and 'traitors', were jailed and executed. In the bloody confrontation between the Islamic government forces and opposition that peaked in 1980–81, many prominent regime figures, such as Ayatollah Beheshti and Prime Minister Ali Raja'i, also lost their lives in a series of bomb explosions carried out by *Mujahideen* and *Feda'iyan* activists. At one point, this cast serious doubt on the survival of the Islamic regime.

The second *jihadi* objective was the creation of a pure and unified Islamic movement under Khomeini's leadership. This involved the marginalization or, in some cases, expunging of those followers of Khomeini who were viewed as undesirable or who had the potential to challenge Khomeini's vision of an Islamic Iran. These included a number of ayatollahs who either doubted the efficacy of Khomeini's approach or found it difficult to agree entirely with his version of political Islam. Grand Ayatollah Mohammad Kazem Shariatmadari, who had saved Khomeini from execution in 1963 and favoured a gentler and more humane application of Islam, was placed under house arrest after denouncing the occupation of the US embassy in Tehran by a group of militant Khomeini supporters in 1979 (discussed in more detail in chapter 4). Bani-Sadr,[12] whom Khomeini had regarded almost as a son, was forced out of presidency into exile in June 1981; his foreign minister, Sadeq Qotbzadeh, was executed in 1982 on charges of plotting against the government. Even Ayatollah Hussein Ali Montazeri, the man initially anointed as Khomeini's successor, was eventually marginalized, with his succession entitlement revoked in 1989.

The third objective was to buttress and secure the two-tier Islamic order. As part of this objective, ordained by Khomeini, three significant organizations were hastily created in 1979. One was the Islamic Republican Party (*Hezb-e Jomhuri-ye Islami*, or IRP), an umbrella organization set up in order to unify a number of political Islamic groups that had sprung into existence either immediately before or soon after the revolution. The most important of these were the Society of Instructors of the Seminaries (*Jame'eh-ye Modarresin Hozeh-ye Elmiyeh*), the Board of the Islamic Coalition (*Hayat-e Mo'talefeh Islami*) and the Islamic Society of Engineers (*Jame'eh-ye Islami Mohandesin*), with the last two representing the *bazaaris* and technocrats. These groups were ideologically analogous to the Society of Combatant Clerics, and were incorporated into the IRP under the latter's leadership. Crystallizing in tandem with the IRP were two other forces – the Organization for Mobilization of the Oppressed (*Sazmane Basiji-e Mostaza'afin*, or simply *Basij*) and the Islamic Revolutionary Guard Corps (*Sepah-e Pasdaran-e Enqelab-e Islami*, IRGC or simply *Sepah*).

The *Basij* was established as a voluntary paramilitary force, made up of young Iranians, recruited and trained from the age of 10 to act as the eyes and ears of the new Islamic regime and maintain internal security, with branches all over Iran under the guidance or control of the regime's clerics. The *Sepah*, on the other hand, was entrusted with a constitutional responsibility to protect the Islamic system, and as such to act as guardian of the system, with extensive powers. Today, membership of the *Basij* is said to number around half a million, and the *Sepah* about 150,000, with the *Basij* working in tandem with or often under the guidance of the *Sepah*, which has grown to be the most powerful and pervasive security actor in the country, with substantial influence in the political, economic and social-cultural life of Iran.

These organizations were established in addition to the military (*artesh*), which was rapidly reconstituted and restructured under a new command, with the task of not only primarily defending Iran's borders, but also playing a critical role in maintaining domestic order when needed. The leaders of all these forces, which gained saliency in the context of the Iran–Iraq War (1980–88), were appointed by the Supreme Leader and owed their loyalty to him. This remains the case today.

To boost and consolidate the regime's clerical hold on the economy and to manage the wealth expropriated from the Shah and those alleged to have been associated with him, the Islamic Republic developed and expanded the system of Islamic foundations (*bonyad*s) in the country.[13] While some *bonyads* had existed prior to the revolution, many in the form of religious endowments *(waqfs)*, the scope and significance of their operations grew dramatically after 1979, with the founding of a number of private and public *bonyads*. While ostensibly non-profit and established to provide social and public services, many *bonyads* are engaged in commercial and financial practices such as banking, trade and manufacturing. Benefiting from immunity from government regulation and tax exemptions, the *bonyads* became an important means whereby the clerics could assume control of various economic and commercial resources and subsequently operate them in conjunction with rich merchants for a variety of purposes, including charitable and humanitarian ones. The *bonyads* remain a key cornerstone of clerical and conservative power in Iran, accounting for 25–35 per cent of the country's gross domestic product by the mid-2000s.[14] They also underpin Iran's 'soft power' as flexible actors outside the Iranian state by funding various humanitarian, educational and cultural projects in different Muslim countries, especially in Iran's neighbourhood.

Among the chief beneficiaries of these newly established systems of patronage were the members of the IRP, the zealous and highly conservative vanguard of the new regime's vision. Although Khomeini disbanded the IRP in 1987, due to his belief that there was no need for a party in an Islamic state and because of internal conflict within the party, it had, initially, been a powerful organization with close ties to the IRGC, the *Basij* and the *artesh*. Together, these groups constituted the most potent forces in the regime's processes of homogenizing and monopolizing power, and defending Iran in the war against Iraq. However, since the abolition of the IRP, a number of other political groupings have become active on the political scene. The IRGC, the *Basij* and the *artesh*, on the other hand, have continued to grow and function largely as the repository of the *jihadi* aspect of Khomeini's approach, with the IRGC assuming a commanding position and enjoying extraordinary privileges.

Khomeini's ijtihadi *dimension*

The *jihadi* policies of the early years of the Islamic regime developed against the backdrop of an intensely hostile international climate. In addition to adversarial relations with the United States, the Islamic Republic was invaded in its infancy by Saddam Hussein's Iraq, plunging the country into the bloody Iran–Iraq War – two issues which will be discussed in detail in chapter 4. In this context, Khomeini had relatively little opportunity to pursue the more reformist aspect of his political ideology. By the second half of the 1980s, however, once Khomeini and his supporters had by and large succeeded in silencing or eliminating their opponents and in consolidating power, the Islamic Republic experienced a shift towards the *ijtihadi* dimension of Khomeini's approach. This heralded Iran's construction as a strong modern and viable Islamic state, capable of defending itself against internal disorder and foreign encroachment.

As noted above, Khomeini had a long history of *ijtihadi* activities. His entire platform of opposition to the Shah had been built on creative interpretations and applications of Islamic principles. He had acted in ways that made him a *mujtahid-e a'lam* – a leading creative interpreter and activist of Islam.[15] While remaining committed to fighting internal and external opposition as well as challenging the legitimacy of the international system of the nation-state with his pan-Islamic universalist stance,[16] Khomeini appears to have become increasingly aware of the impossibility of building an enduring and formidable Islamic state on *jihadi* principles alone. The system of government he had put in place contained an in-built elasticity that allowed for a degree of political pluralism and foreign policy flexibility to facilitate wider public participation in the policymaking and policy implementation processes. This elasticity began to make itself felt in 1983–84, when a major metamorphosis in Iran's political structures opened the door for an eventual diversification of the Islamic leadership. While holding the reins firmly from above, Khomeini allowed this transformation to take place, which resulted in the emergence of three broad political clusters by the late 1980s, as canvassed in chapter 1.

The first was the *jihadi*, or revolutionary/conservative, cluster, which had already coalesced around such figures as Mahdavi Kani and Khamenei. From the start, this cluster had managed to gain hold of most of the instruments of state power and resources on the pretext of combating 'enemies' of the revolution (and, by extension, Islam). It therefore succeeded in securing a dominant and active role in the conduct of the Islamic Republic's domestic and foreign policies. This cluster generally argued for the strengthening of the Islamic order, the preservation of a traditional mode of life, the promotion of national self-sufficiency, ideological and cultural purity, and an uncompromising approach to the United States and its allies, particularly Israel.

The second was the *ijtihadi*, the reformist and internationalist cluster, which began to evolve in 1987

The Islamic Order

around such prominent figures as Mehdi Karroubi and Mohammad Khatami, both distinguished clerical supporters of Khomeini. Karroubi was a moderate Islamist democracy activist and a former chairman and founding member of the Assembly of Combative Clerics (*Majma-e Ruhaniyun-e Mobarez*, ACC) who subsequently served twice as speaker of the *Majles* (1989–92, 2000–04), before running for office in the 2005 and 2009 presidential elections. He has come to be recognized as a vocal critic of the Council of Guardians and the Islamic judicial system in the way it was instituted. Khatami was a reformist Islamist scholar,[17] who served as Minister of Culture and Islamic Guidance (1982–92), before being elected as president in two subsequent landslide elections (1997 and 2005). The *ijtihadi* cluster called for increased pluralism and democracy within the overarching framework of an Islamic political system.[18] Some of its leading figures, most importantly Khatami, discreetly favoured the promotion of Islamic civil society, the relaxation of social controls, economic openness, a cultural renaissance and a more reconciliatory foreign policy approach. Members of the cluster drew inspiration from such Iranian thinkers as Ali Shari'ati (1933–77) and Abdul Karim Soroush, who blended Islamic with Western Enlightenment ideas to argue for a democratic Islamic society.[19]

The third was the *amalgaran*, the centralist or pragmatist cluster, which crystallized around Rafsanjani. This entity stood between the first two clusters and organized itself within two parties – the Executives of Construction Party (*Hezb-e Kargozaran-e Sazandegi*), which endorsed the reformist line on culture, and the Justice and Development Party (*Hezb-E'tedal va Tose'eh*), which tended to be more conservative on cultural issues. This camp showed an interest in economic modernization and trade liberalization, but was less concerned with democratization and social reform.[20]

Initially, Khomeini appeared to be quite comfortable with this degree of political pluralism, so long as it gave no signs of threatening his Islamic vision and order. Yet when factionalism began to break out among the ranks, Khomeini reversed his position, arguing that the prevention of disagreement within the Islamic state was a religious duty incumbent on all Muslims, and abolished the IRP in 1987.[21] He declared Iran to be a non-partisan Islamic state, but didn't succeed in putting an end to factionalism.[22] Nevertheless, developments in the late 1980s encouraged Khomeini's *ijtihadi* reformist supporters to become more active on the political scene. In March 1988, a number of them formed the ACC under the leadership of Karroubi and with strong support from Khatami.

The post-Khomeini period

By the time of his death on 3 June 1989, Khomeini had not only entrenched his *jihadi* programme, but also initiated an *ijtihadi* dimension in Iranian politics. Khamenei and Rafsanjani, two of his closest loyalists, were now more than ever thrust into the limelight, with the first replacing Khomeini as Supreme Leader and the second becoming president. However, Khamenei, even more than Khomeini before him, became the source and focus of much controversy within the Iranian clerical establishment. Many grand ayatollahs were sceptical of his credentials, as Khamenei had only held a middling rank in the Shi'ite clerical hierarchy as *hojjat-ol-eslam* (Authority on Islam), which under the Constitution disqualified him from taking up the post of Supreme Leader. He was hastily promoted to the rank of Ayatollah in 1989 and took up the position.[23] In view of Khamenei's clerical standing, the charismatic and capable President Rafsanjani, who played a key role in the elevation of Khamenei, became the prominent figure in politics.

During Rafsanjani's presidency (1989–97), Iranian politics shifted from an initial approach of pragmatic accommodation and compromise to one of competition and deadlock.[24] Rafsanjani commenced his term with a promise of domestic and foreign policy openness in order to alleviate the suffering of the Iranian people under the conditions of the Iran–Iraq War austerity measures, US economic sanctions and Islamic centralization of power. He had already succeeded in persuading Khomeini that the war with Iraq had reached a point where it was threatening the Islamic Revolution and therefore the time had come to accept a United Nations (UN) proposed ceasefire. Until that point, Khomeini had vehemently resisted a ceasefire, and had demanded that the UN declare Iraq the aggressor, and that Iraq should pay war reparations of US$150 billion, release all Iranian war prisoners and withdraw to pre-war borders. However, he ultimately found it expedient to accept Rafsanjani's reasoning. He agreed in mid-1988 to an unconditional ceasefire under UN Council Resolution 598, whose signing he compared to drinking 'a cup of poison'.[25] Both Baghdad and Tehran claimed victory – a victory that marked a stalemate rather than a peace agreement.

Even so, the end of active conflict, which had severely impeded the reconstruction dimension of Khomeini's vision and had taken a very heavy toll on the Iranian people, helped Rafsanjani to instigate a degree of economic freedom and some foreign policy gestures. Whilst showing little interest in political reform, he essentially remained focused on consolidation and continuity of the Islamic regime, improving economic conditions and seeking to promote the Islamic regime to a level of cordiality within the world order. He scored some success on these fronts, as he promoted the idea and establishment of several free economic zones, widened trade with Russia, India and China, and assured neighbouring Gulf Cooperation Council states of Iran's desire for improved relations. He also visited Saudi Arabia, whose relations with Iran under Khomeini had been extremely hostile, on a goodwill mission.

Rafsanjani also downplayed the role of the Iranian state in the execution of Khomeini's *fatwa* (religious ruling) that called for the killing of the British Indian novelist, Salman Rushdie, whose book *The Satanic Verses* was considered by Khomeini to be a blasphemous insult to Islam.[26] Moreover, Rafsanjani used Iran's influence to secure the release of some of the Western hostages detained by Iran's Hezbollah (Party of God) allies in Lebanon. In so doing, he signalled to the West a possibility for better relations – to which he received no encouraging response, especially from Washington. Ultimately, Rafsanjani, who had never intended to rock the boat in any way, could not achieve much more than keeping Iran afloat and slightly improving its regional and international standing. The *jihadis'* dominance of the power structure and their emphasis on ideological purity as a means to govern prevailed. Along with this, patronage, corruption, administrative dysfunctionality, moral lapses and poor governance continued on an upward trajectory.

While the end of the Iran–Iraq War and Khomeini's death had generated some space for Rafsanjani to engage in some pragmatic policies, these very developments also removed the variables that had held the different political Islamist clusters together. Khomeini's departure put an end to all semblance of political unity between the formerly cooperative clusters. From early in his presidency, Rafsanjani had shown himself willing to cooperate with the dominant *jihadi* faction in order to achieve his pragmatist goals. However, it soon became clear that Rafsanjani could expect no support for his economic liberalization agenda from the hardliners, who resisted his pragmatism with growing strength and efficacy. As a result, Rafsanjani found himself treading an increasingly fine line between the *jihadi* and *ijtihadi* factions. A majority of Iranians experienced no tangible positive change in their living conditions and, by the end of his second term, Rafsanjani found himself forced into an ever-tighter political corner. He consequently made efforts to ingratiate himself with the emerging *ijtihadi* faction.[27] While too late to reverse his personal political fortune, it created an opening for the forces of reform and for the ascension of reformist Khatami.

Khatami's Islamic democracy

Khatami assumed office in an electoral landslide in 1997 with the firm conviction that the time had come to transform Iran from a political culture of *jihad* to *ijtihad*. Working within the framework of the Constitution and within the Islamic framework laid down by Khomeini, he called for domestic political reforms that would promote 'Islamic civil society' as a precondition for, and in tandem with, 'Islamic democracy'. Khatami showed an acute awareness of the fact that the longevity of the Islamic regime and Iran's economic prosperity and social-cultural progress depended on the loosening of political and social control in favour of wider public participation, freedom of thought and expression and greater room for individual initiative and creativity, as well as constructive engagement within an increasingly interdependent world.

From 1997 until 2001, Khatami set in motion a gradual process of reform that won the support of a large majority of Iranians. He was very comfortably elected for a second term, with his supporters also dominating the *Majles*. Yet Khatami faced growing resistance from the conservative Islamic factions. Although he maintained reasonably good working relations with Khamenei and vigorously sought to avoid open confrontation with the *jihadi* forces, the latter precipitously grew weary of Khatami's reforms. Concerned about the impact of Khatami's moves on his power, authority and conservative ideological stance, Khamenei refrained from providing the degree of backing that Khatami needed in order to overcome his *jihadi* opponents' obstructionism. Khatami's reform efforts were impeded and blocked by the conservative factions almost every step of the way. These factions, with dominance of virtually all the consequential instruments of state power, had developed a deep vested interest in the existing system and remained opposed to changes that could affect their hold on power and privileged status.

This situation was not helped by the fact that, for all his reformist efforts, Khatami received no more than lip service from the United States and its major European allies, which continued to view Khatami and his reformist supporters as powerless and incapable of prevailing over the conservative factions. While the European powers maintained a cautious policy of 'constructive engagement' towards the Islamic regime, largely to preserve their individual lucrative trade deals with Iran, the US administration of President Bill Clinton made no more than largely superficial gestures in response to Khatami's reforms. It lifted sanctions on the import of a few insignificant items, such as pistachios and caviar, and called for a road map to move forward, without giving anything that could provide for confidence-building measures. Under heavy lobbying from the American Israel Public Affairs Committee, the Clinton administration committed itself to a policy of 'dual containment' of Iran and Iraq, despite the fact that it became increasingly clear over a period of time that it was not working.[28] The policy was heavily criticized by several senior American political figures, including Zbigniew Brzezinski and Brent Scowcroft, former National Security Advisors to ex-Presidents Jimmy Carter and George H. Bush, respectively.[29]

Washington continued to accuse Iran of supporting international terrorism and developing a nuclear programme for military purposes. It ignored the Khatami government's insistence that the country's programme was for peaceful purposes. Iran's nuclear programme had started under the Shah, with German expertise and construction as well as America's blessing.[30] Although halted for several years, the Islamic regime resumed the programme after the war with Iraq. From 1989 to 2005, Khatami's top nuclear negotiator with the International Atomic Energy Agency (IAEA) and three European powers – the UK, France and Germany – was Dr Hassan Rouhani, a moderate whose 2013 election to the presidency, position and policies are discussed in chapter 4. In an attempt to open a window for improved relations with the United States and to assuage Western concerns about Iran's nuclear programme, the Khatami leadership engaged in a number of policy actions to which Washington could have responded positively but did not. The Khatami administration loudly condemned the 11 September 2001 al-Qaeda terrorist attacks on the United States and fully cooperated with the United States at the Bonn Conference on Afghanistan, which endorsed the formation of the internationally backed government of Hamid Karzai and the interventionist role of the UN and the United States in the country. In addition, the head of the Iranian delegation at the conference, the current and highly able foreign minister Mohammad Javad Zarif, signalled a strong desire to his American counterpart, James Dobbins, to open the way to settle Iranian–US differences. But Dobbins's communication to Washington in this respect fell on deaf ears.[31]

Subsequently, in order to demonstrate that Iran had no military nuclear objectives, the Khatami government instituted a temporary suspension to Iran's uranium enrichment and in December 2003 signed an 'Additional Protocol' to Iran's existing Nuclear Non-Proliferation Treaty safeguard agreement with the IAEA, which granted the agency's inspectors greater authority in verifying Iran's nuclear programme. Even a December 2003 US intelligence agency report, entitled *Iran: Nuclear Intentions and Capabilities*, stated: 'We judge with high confidence that in fall, 2003, Tehran halted its nuclear weapons program ... [and] we do not know whether it currently intends to develop nuclear weapons' – something that the former US Secretary of Defense, Robert Gates, subsequently described as a 'grievous blow' to US policy towards Iran at the time.[32]

Yet none of these measures seemed to cut any ice with the United States, its major European allies, or Israel, which has never ceased to accuse Iran of having a secret military programme to produce nuclear bombs.

If anything, US hostility to the Iranian government intensified after 11 September. President George W. Bush condemned Iran, along with Syria and North Korea, as part of an 'axis of evil', and therefore liable to be punished by the United States. This unexpected rebuff put Khatami and his reformist supporters on the defensive against their conservative opponents and left them vulnerable to the latter's accusation of 'sleeping with the enemy', thus preventing them from taking any further steps towards improved relations. This, together with Khatami's inability to fulfil his promise of reforms to the extent necessary, dealt a serious blow to the reformist camp, as many of those, especially the youth, who today form more than 50 per cent of Iran's 77 million population, became disillusioned with the reformists, widening the arena for the conservatives to become more assertive.[33]

As a consequence, in 2005 the conservatives re-emerged as the dominant cluster in the *Majles*. The IRG became the 'praetorian guard' for the conservatives, and Iranian politics shifted to the right. This culminated in the election of former mayor of Tehran from the ranks of the conservatives, Mahmoud Ahmadinejad, to the presidency in June 2005.

Ahmadinejad's presidency

Ahmadinejad was a relatively unknown figure in Iranian politics until his rise to the presidency.[34] He came from an unsophisticated, non-clerical, poor and rural socioeconomic background. Although a staunch follower of Khomeini, he played no leading role in the Iranian revolution. However, after the revolution, he gained close identification with the *jihadi* cluster. He joined the *Sepah* and served in its intelligence and security apparatus in the 1980s. This had enabled him to develop some links with the security establishment. He was educated as an engineer to doctoral level and served as a teacher for a while, before assuming administrative/political positions in a couple of Iranian provinces, culminating in his appointment as governor of the province of Ardabil in 1993. Khatami had removed him from that position in 1997, leading him back to his teaching career.

He had, nonetheless, emerged as the main leader of a coalition of conservative groups called the Alliance of Builders of Islamic Iran (*E'telaf-e Abadgaran-e Iran-e Islam-e*) in opposition to Khatami's domestic reforms and foreign policy openings, which he thought were compromising Khomeini's Islamic vision and were making Iran vulnerable to Western (especially American and Israeli) influence. The Alliance had provided him with a political power base, resulting in his appointment by the City Council of Tehran as mayor in 2003, which gave him a platform from which he gained wider visibility. He had all along viewed himself as representing Khomeini's class of *mostaz'afin* (the downtrodden). His conservatism was very much influenced by Ayatollah Mohammad Mesbah Yazdi, an influential and powerful hardline cleric and member of the Assembly of Experts, who was strongly opposed to any form of democratic rule and reform movement.

Since under the Iranian Constitution Khatami could not run for more than two terms, Ahmadinejad contested the presidential election from the conservative camp against Rafsanjani, who once again thought that his centralist pragmatism could bridge the gap between the reformists and conservatives, and enable him to secure the presidency for the second time. However, Rafsanjani's image had been substantially tarnished as one who had been accused of having enriched himself and his family with lucrative businesses, built a monopoly in the Iranian pistachio industry and allowed patronage and corruption to flourish during his previous presidency. In a victory that surprised both Iranian and international observers, Ahmadinejad won 62 per cent of the votes cast in the presidential election, followed by the conservatives' win in the parliamentary elections – a major victory for the *jihadi* cluster and a serious setback for pragmatists and reformists.[35]

During his first term, Ahmadinejad worked in tandem with Khamenei to consolidate the *jihadis'* hold on power. Claiming that the United States and its allies, especially Israel, were determined to destroy the Islamic regime, he focused predominantly on four issues: ingratiating himself with the *mostaz'afin*, especially in the rural areas, which he visited more frequently than any of his predecessors and where he broke bread with families to build his reputation as a pious Shi'a and devoted disciple of Khomeini; building Iran's military power and nuclear programme; maintaining and strengthening support for Iran's partners, including Syria, Lebanon's Hezbollah and some powerful Shi'a factions in Iraq;[36] and widening relations with some like-minded or friendly Third World states such as Venezuela, Brazil, Zimbabwe and Malaysia. He focused on the latter issue with an emphasis on strengthening the Non-Aligned Movement (NAM), leading to Tehran hosting the movement's sixteenth summit in August 2012. All this resonated with Khomeini's anti-imperialist stance for oppressed peoples in the world, suited the conservatives' agenda and conformed to Khamenei's stance. The NAM summit, which was presided over by Khamenei and in which 120 countries participated, was promoted as a means not only to display Iran as a paramount actor on the world stage, but also to act as a counterweight to the US-led sanctions and pressure.

The *jihadi* faction's dominance in all governmental branches prompted an effective merger between the reformist and pragmatic factions, as both viewed Ahmadinejad's policies as detrimental to the country. They found the president's populist, ad hoc approach to Iran's social and economic development alarming. Those policies involved wealth redistribution through salary and subsidy increases, as well as pet projects and cash handouts, especially in rural areas. This, along with state patronage of selected groups and institutions that were important to the preservation of the regime under the conservatives, generated little sustainable development, administrative efficiency or clean and effective governance.

Unlike Khatami and Rafsanjani, Ahmadinejad adopted an assertive and frequently confrontationist policy attitude towards the West, and established camaraderie with those heads of state, such as the late Venezuelan President Hugo Chavez and Zimbabwean leader Robert Mugabe, who displayed a particular distaste for the United States and some of its allies, Israel in particular.[37] In general, he pursued a policy of uncompromising isolation that led him to shun all foreign investment in favour of national self-sufficiency. He frequently castigated the United States as an evil power and Israel as an aggressive 'Zionist state', questioning the legitimacy of Israel's existence and branding the Holocaust as a Zionist ploy. He appointed a hardline conservative, Saeed Jalili, as his deputy foreign minister and chief nuclear negotiator, and adopted a defiant stance on Iran's nuclear programme.[38]

Ahmadinejad's policies caused Iran to become even more isolated from the international community and brought about three rounds of UN sanctions and increasingly crippling American and European financial and economic sanctions, especially from mid-2012. This, in conjunction with increasing corruption, fraud and inefficiency in governmental operations as well as a chronically underdeveloped taxation system, caused the Iranian economy to slide into stagnation. This was despite the fact that Iran has had the third largest oil and second largest gas reserves in the world, and that its annual oil and gas exports, which make up 80 per cent of the country's total export earnings and 60 to 70 per cent of the Iranian government's revenue, rose substantially between 2008 and 2011, amounting to US$75–US$95 billion per year, due to an increase in international demand and continued Middle East volatility. Yet the financial and economic mismanagement under Ahmadinejad contributed substantially to rising inflation and unemployment. The country's annual economic growth declined progressively from 8 per cent in 2007 to 3.2 per cent in 2009. Unemployment became particularly acute among those aged 16–25.[39] In 2012, Iran's official inflation rate was estimated to be 23.6 per cent and its unemployment rate 15.5 per cent, although the real rates for both were probably around 30–40 per cent and increasing as Western sanctions accelerated. The value of Iran's currency, the rial, was at 50 per cent of what it was in 2010. This was all despite the government's attempts to institute a programme of phasing out food and fuel subsidies, the first stage of which occurred in December 2010, but the subsequent phases were delayed for fear of more public disquiet.

Ahmadinejad's successor, Rouhani, subsequently claimed that 'Iran's oil and gas export incomes during Ahmadinejad's two-term presidency reached some $800 billion, and his administration had spent some $640 billion of that on importing goods until March 2013'. Rouhani criticized Ahmadinejad for abusing around US$100 billion of the country's annual revenue.[40] One of Ahmadinejad's important pet projects was the *Maskan-e Mehr* housing project, designed to build 600,000 low-income homes across Iran. However, the cheap credit that 'he used to fund *Maskan-e Mehr* had a devastating impact on the economy. It was emblematic of his approach to economic policy: populist, redistributive initiatives turn into a herd of white elephants.'[41]

As public discontent with the Islamic government soared during Ahmadinejad's first term, the reformist and pragmatist factional leaders could not approve of Ahmadinejad's policy behaviour. They decided to oppose him in the June 2009 presidential election. Mir-Hussein Mousavi, who had served as Iran's prime minister for five years during the war with Iraq, and Karroubi, as mentioned earlier, a prominent cleric, former Speaker of the *Majles* and previous contender for the presidency, ran against Ahmadinejad from the reformist-pragmatist camp and were publicly supported by Khatami and Rafsanjani – that is, the high-profile leaders of both the reformist and the pragmatist clusters. However, the election turned out to be highly controversial, as Ahmadinejad was declared the winner amidst widespread allegations of vote-rigging.

The election results provoked a showdown between the *jihadis* and the pragmatist-reformist coalition. Leading figures in the coalition, including Khatami, Mousavi, Karroubi and Rafsanjani, publicly turned against the government. They condemned Ahmadinejad's election as 'fraudulent'. Since Khamenei had declared Ahmadinejad's win to be a 'blessing from God' before the customary declaration of the results by the Council of Guardians, they also indirectly challenged the wisdom and authority of the Supreme Leader. The government countered peaceful mass protests, unseen since the revolution, with a bloody crackdown, killing dozens of people and arresting hundreds more. Khamenei branded the protestors as foreign-instigated enemies of the Islamic Republic. Mousavi and Karroubi were put under house arrest, where they remain to date, although under less severe conditions.

Some 100 opposition figures, including Khatami's former vice-president, Mohammad-Ali Abtahi – a member (like Khatami and Karroubi) of the Central Council of the Association of Combative Clerics (*Majma'-e Rouhaniyun-e Mobaraz*) which was established in 1988 – and former Deputy Foreign Minister Mohsen Aminzadeh – a founding member of the reformist party, the Islamic Iran Participation Front (*Jebhe-ye Mosharekat Iran-i Islami*), which was founded in 1998 and is led by Mohammad Reza Khatami, former President Khatami's brother – were thrown into gaol. Abtahi was released within a year after making a public confession of wrongdoing, which many claimed was made under duress, and Aminzadeh was kept in prison until he was transferred to a hospital for treatment in 2012. Khamenei's handling of the situation made him appear to be no less of an autocrat than the Shah in the eyes of many Iranians. The split between the *jihadis* and *ijtihadis* and the disconnect between the 'sovereignty of God' and the 'sovereignty of people' were now so public and deep that they seriously threatened the legitimacy of the regime.

By and large, Iranian politics during Ahmadinejad's two terms witnessed 'a progressive shift of the Iranian Revolution from popular republicanism to absolute theocratic sovereignty'.[42] Yet the 2009 election also highlighted a second schism within the conservative faction itself. The Supreme Leader and several powerful elements, most notably the faction of the *Majles* Speaker Ali Larijani, moved to limit Ahmadinejad's autonomy and tighten their hold on state power. Aware of these machinations, the president made some overtures towards the *ijtihadi* and pragmatist clusters. Between 2009 and 2012, several clear signs of dissent within the conservative cluster surfaced, with a split between the ultra-conservatives, who emphasized the Islamic character of the polity and rallied behind Khamenei, and those who backed Ahmadinejad's Iranian-Islamic nationalist rhetoric. By 2012, the rift between the Supreme Leader and the President had widened to the extent that neither appeared able to trust the other amidst a complete breakdown of communication. This was reflected in Khamenei's growing tendency to intervene in Ahmadinejad's political decisions. For instance, when Ahmadinejad dismissed the Minister of Intelligence Heydar Moslehi in April 2011, the Supreme Leader reinstated him.[43] At one point the President disappeared for two weeks without any explanation, although it was rumoured in Tehran that he was securing a 'dirt file' on the Supreme Leader's son, Mojtaba. The latter, who had backed Ahmadinejad in the 2009 election, but had subsequently grown disillusioned with him, is said to be a hardliner cleric with ambitions to succeed his father. He is also reported to preside over a huge amount of wealth, much of it allegedly gained through illicit activities.[44]

Whatever the truth of this matter, despite Ahmadinejad's efforts to build a network of supporters within the Islamic system, he could never counter the Supreme Leader's control of the very organs of state power that grew and became more powerful during the period of his presidency. The *Sepah* and its affiliate *Basij*, the *bonyads* and the *artesh*, all of whose leaders are appointed by the Supreme Leader and owe their loyalty to him, continue to exercise greater and increasing influence in the political, economic and social life of Iran. Among these forces, the *Sepah* especially emerged in a more powerful and pervasive role in the Iranian polity during and after Ahmadinejad's presidency than ever before.

By the end of Ahmadinejad's second term, Iran was in a dire situation. It suffered from severe stagflation, an almost depleted national treasury, crippling sanctions, growing discord between its two tiers of government, and more power in the hands of coercive organs of the state. The country was also deeply embroiled in costly operations in the Syrian conflict, providing increasing financial, economic and military assistance to Iran's only Arab strategic ally, the regime of Bashar al-Assad, against its opponents, and in maintaining Iran's proxy Hezbollah force in Lebanon, while facing the threat of military action from Israel and the United States over its nuclear programme. The scene was once again set for the Iranian political pendulum to swing back towards the *ijtihadi* component, which had been marginalized under Ahmadinejad.

4

Rouhani's Presidency and US–Iranian Relations

Against the backdrop of a panorama of issues and challenges, Iran held its tenth presidential election on 14 June 2013 to replace Mahmoud Ahmadinejad. Once again this set the scene for a shift in the Islamic regime's domestic and foreign policy postures. While the Supreme Leader and his supporters might have preferred the election of a conservative, it had also become clear to them that the Iranian electorate had never been more deeply and widely disillusioned with conservative rule. This time, therefore, they found it expedient to allow the election results to reflect the will of the people, a strategy viewed as the most effective way to dampen public discontent and ease Western pressure on the country. Of the ten original presidential candidates, including one conservative and one reformist who dropped out prior to the election, the reformist and pragmatist-backed moderate cleric, Hassan Rouhani, achieved a landslide victory. Rouhani had campaigned on a platform of moderation, anti-extremism and reform in the conduct of Iran's domestic and foreign affairs. His victory surprised those who had expected a tinkering of the results in favour of one of the conservative candidates, particularly Saeed Jalili, Ahmadinejad's former deputy foreign minister and chief nuclear negotiator.

Since assuming power in August 2013, Rouhani has had to pursue two imperatives simultaneously and interactively: political and socioeconomic reforms as well as the negotiated lifting of Western sanctions. This has meant that he has had to rely on foreign policy breakthroughs, especially with the United States, in order to score success on the domestic front, while also giving Iran a new foreign policy direction. The task has been difficult and laborious, but not necessarily insurmountable.

This chapter evaluates the origins and nature of Iran's adversarial relations with the United States and its allies, specifically Israel, in the context of three overriding themes. The first is the entrenchment of a pattern of mutual demonization that developed in both the United States and Iran in the aftermath of the Iranian revolution. The second is the self-reinforcing connection between US–Iranian hostility on the one hand, and the mutual persistence and legitimization of the hardline conservative agendas in Iran and the United States against one another, on the other. This dynamic has posed serious difficulties for the forces of moderation on either side to promote the need for two-way accommodation. The third theme is internal resistance, for a mixture of pragmatic and ideological reasons, to reconciliation at the political level in both Iran and the United States, which has nevertheless been punctuated by moments of political opportunity and pragmatism. Understanding how these patterns of mutual suspicion and hostility have come to encapsulate US–Iranian relations is critical to comprehending both the nature of these relations today and the prospects for improvement in the future. It is only against

73

a background that one can evaluate Rouhani's
:ulties and achievements so far, which will form
⸺ :ocus of the second half of this chapter.

Contrasting legacies

As noted in chapter 2, the story of the souring of
US–Iranian relations began with the CIA-orchestrated
fall in 1953 of Mohammad Mossadeq on the Iranian
side and was clinched on the American side by the
political demise of Mohammad Reza Shah Pahlavi.
For the United States, the Shah's overthrow in 1979
was a significant political and geostrategic blow and
a bitter humiliation. Since the CIA's reinstalment of
the Shah on his throne in 1953, the US government
had remained the Shah's primary international backer
within a largely, but occasionally fluctuating, patron-
client relationship. The pro-Western, secular monarch
was seen as an invaluable ally against the Soviet Union
in the context of Cold War rivalry and was treated
accordingly.[1] Under the Shah, Iran's political neutrality was compromised as its national autonomy was
progressively subsumed by the strategic calculations of
the United States, which viewed the country as a frontline state and critical to America's policy of containing
Soviet communism.

The revolution of 1978/79 generated enormous con-
fusion and anger in Washington. While continuing
to reassure the Shah of their unwavering support, US
officials and policymakers were conflicted over how to
approach the crisis. Paralysed by division and unwill-
ing to instigate a repeat of 1953, the US government
nevertheless held faith with the Shah and refused,
from the outset, to engage in dialogue with Ruhollah

Khomeini, whom President Jimmy Carter was quick to label as 'nutty'.[2]

From the Iranian perspective, things could not have been more different. The overthrow of the Shah, who was denounced as the 'lackey' or 'crony' of the Americans, represented a nationalist and religious victory over the United States as a hegemonic imperialist power. This, together with built-up resentment over alleged US complicity in the human rights abuses perpetrated under the Shah, gave a definitively anti-American, Islamic tone to the revolutionary rhetoric. Khomeini strongly echoed this sentiment by referring to Carter as 'Yezid', the Islamic ruler responsible for the murder of Imam Hussein, the third Imam and one of the main martyrs in Shi'a Islam. This was also a label that Khomeini had applied to the Shah.[3]

The hostage crisis

Deterioration in US–Iranian relations was virtually inevitable in the context from which the revolution emerged. The future course of the US–Iranian relationship, however, was set much more strongly by the events surrounding the Iran hostage crisis. The crisis began on 4 November 1979, when a pro-Khomeini group of Iranian students stormed the US embassy in Tehran and seized 52 American staff as hostages. It ended 444 days later, on 20 January 1981, when Ronald Reagan replaced Carter as president of the United States. The episode, which Carter viewed as a result of terrorism and anarchy, was a source of humiliation for the US government and of shock and outrage for the American public. In Iran, the news of the embassy takeover was greeted with elation, as a moment of triumph for the Islamic revolutionary spirit over the 'Great Satan' that could be shown to the world. The crisis was severely exacerbated by existing patterns of mutual incomprehension and demonization, at both the political and the ideological levels.

The motives of the hostage-takers have been widely debated.[4] Nevertheless, the US decision (for which the Shah's good friend, former US Secretary of State Henry Kissinger lobbied hard) to allow the Shah to enter the United States for medical treatment on 22 October 1979 was clearly a decisive factor. This, together with a failed military attempt to rescue the hostages, generated fears of a US conspiracy to overthrow the Islamic regime in Iran in a repeat of 1953. Washington's actions further fuelled anti-American sentiment in the country and galvanized the Iranian public. While the hostage-takers seem to have acted without direct instruction from the Islamic leadership, Khomeini was quick to endorse the students' actions and to use the episode for his own political purposes. The crisis provided the Islamic Republic with an opportunity to demean the United States, to mobilize and radicalize the Iranian population under Khomeini's leadership, and to expunge the more liberal elements of the Iranian leadership, such as Prime Minister Mehdi Bazargan and his Foreign Minister Ibrahim Yazdi, who denounced the takeover and sought to negotiate with the Americans.

In Washington, on the other hand, the crisis helped cement an image of the Islamic Republic as 'fundamentalist' and therefore irrational and fanatical. Khomeini's unwillingness to negotiate with US representatives fed into a perception that reason and dialogue with the Islamic Republic were completely useless. The United States responded by adopting a hardline posture, severing diplomatic ties with Iran on 7 April 1980 and imposing a number of economic and military sanctions in the ensuing months. The hostage crisis exacerbated anxiety about and bitterness over the 'loss' of Iran as a significant geostrategic asset in the Middle East. To compensate for this loss, the United States sought to expand its influence among Iran's neighbours – the Gulf Arab states (including Iraq), and Egypt and Turkey in particular – under the aegis of what became known as the Carter Doctrine. Its successor, the Reagan Doctrine, which envisaged pre-positioning of American military hardware and a 'rapid deployment force' in the Gulf to nip in the bud any imminent danger from anti-US forces,[5] went further than the Carter Doctrine, instigating an American–Iranian strategic rivalry in the region.

The Iran–Iraq War

The consequences of this shift in US foreign policy became apparent when, on 22 September 1980, in the middle of the hostage crisis, the Islamic Republic was invaded by Iraq under the orders of the Iraqi dictator, Saddam Hussein. With Iran in the midst of post-revolutionary turmoil and an international diplomatic crisis, Saddam had calculated a swift and easy victory that would result, at a minimum, in the annexation of the Arab-majority, strategically valuable, oil-rich province of Khuzestan and, at a maximum, in the toppling of Khomeini's government and the establishment of Iraq as the dominant regional power.

Instead, the invasion plunged both countries into the longest, bloodiest and most costly war in the modern history of the Middle East.[6] Saddam depicted the war as a battle between the forces of secular nationalism and religious fanaticism, carried out in defence of the entire 'Arab nation'. The Islamic Republic, by contrast,

77

presented the conflict as a war to defend Islam against its manifold enemies. Most of the Arab states, more importantly the wealthy oil-rich ones in the Gulf, led by Saudi Arabia, rallied behind Saddam, backing his war effort with massive financial and logistical support. Millions of young Iranians, inspired by a fusion of revolutionary ideology and Shi'ite traditions of martyrdom – as well as a significant number who simply wanted to defend their country despite ambivalence to the new government – volunteered and were killed as the Islamic Republic resorted to human wave tactics to combat the technologically superior Iraqi forces.

From around 1983, the United States began to provide substantial support to the Iraqi war effort.[7] Donald Rumsfeld, who subsequently became US Secretary of Defense (2001–06) and presided over the 2003 US invasion of Iraq, visited Saddam as President Reagan's emissary to convey a message of goodwill and cooperation. Even when Iraq's shocking human rights violations – such as the indiscriminate use of chemical weapons against Iraqi Kurds – were revealed later in the 1980s, the United States and many of its European allies chose not to condemn it, remaining steadfast in their support for Saddam against Khomeini's regime. Such support continued virtually unabated until the Iraqi invasion of Kuwait in August 1990, which was quickly and decisively repulsed by US-led military forces and prompted the United States to begin treating Saddam as a dangerous enemy.

The United States' support for Saddam as a Sunni Arab bulwark against Khomeini's Shi'a government in the context of the Iran–Iraq War contributed to a realignment of regional loyalties, cementing American–Iranian, Arab–Persian and Sunni–Shi'a antagonisms.[8]

The last of these was also exacerbated by Iran's attempts to spread its Islamic revolution abroad.[9] While the Iranian leadership hoped that its revolutionary Islamic message would resonate with some marginalized Sunnis, its impact was in practice limited to Shi'ites. The most striking success of Iran's revolutionary proselytizing was the creation of Hezbollah, the Lebanese Shi'a militant group that would eventually establish itself as one of the region's dominant anti-Israel and anti-US political and military forces.[10] Iran's efforts generated enormous anxiety among the Gulf Arab states, particularly those with substantial but marginalized Shi'a populations. They prompted Saudi Arabia, Bahrain, Kuwait, the United Arab Emirates, Qatar and Oman to form the Gulf Cooperation Council (GCC) as a defensive organization and to support Iraq in the war with Iran.

While Khomeini, from the outset, had declared the Islamic government's foreign policy to be neither pro-Western nor pro-Eastern, but totally 'Islamic', he was ultimately compelled to adopt a more compromising stance. As a result, his rhetorical calls for the export of revolutionary Islam were often countered by pragmatic Iranian foreign policies. An example of this was Iran's strategic partnership with Syria, which forged an alliance between Tehran and the secular Alawite-dominated Ba'athist regime of Hafez al-Assad, primarily to secure Damascus's support in the war against Iraq and to secure a regional Arab ally.[11] In the early years of the war with Iraq, Iran also accepted military aid from Soviet Russia and, indirectly and controversially, purchased arms from Israel, which had an interest in seeing the conflict continue for as long as possible.[12]

The Americans were also capable of compromising their absolute ideological stance in moments of crisis.

This was demonstrated in 1986 when the Iran-Contra scandal broke out. At this time, it was revealed that the US government had been selling weapons to the Iranian government in exchange for the release of American hostages held by Hezbollah militants in Lebanon. The arms-for-hostages deal resulted in the transfer of large quantities of anti-tank and anti-missile technology to the Iranians, in violation of the United States' own arms embargo.[13]

The post-Khomeini era

US–Iranian relations in the 1980s were characterized by unmitigated hostility at the level of discourse that was occasionally punctuated by pragmatism at the level of action. The Islamic Republic found itself surrounded by a hostile international environment and locked into a conflict with Iraq that threatened its very existence. This existential threat and Washington's courting of Saddam lent credibility to the *jihadi* ideology and reinforced the image of a pure Islamic Republic confronted by the universal hostility of a corrupted, materialist world, a rhetoric that built on the Shi'ite culture of persecution and martyrdom.[14] The radicalism of the Islamic Republic helped to justify the United States' demonization of the Iranian Islamic regime as too fanatical to hold a place in the international order. Conversely, Washington's rejectionist attitude towards the Iranian Islamic regime invited Tehran's continued demonization of the United States as its own archenemy and its condemnation of Israel as an aggressive, expansionist American-backed Zionist entity.

The end of the Iran–Iraq War in mid-1988, precipitated by a stalemate and by Khomeini's reluctant decision to accept a ceasefire as a 'bitter pill' for the sake of national salvation, opened the arena for the assertion of pragmatist and reformist ideas in Iranian politics. The election of Hashemi Rafsanjani to the presidency in February 1989, as noted in chapter 3, reflected this trend. Despite intense hostility from the *jihadi* cluster, which viewed reconciliation with the United States as tantamount to a betrayal of the revolution, Rafsanjani sought to improve relations between the two countries, particularly on the economic front. He made several overtures to Washington with the aim of expanding trade and, controversially, reopening Iran's oil industry to foreign companies. Rafsanjani's reorienting of Iran's foreign posture to one of positive neutrality was welcomed by the Arab monarchies in the Gulf. This included Saudi Arabia, the state that had been denounced by Khomeini as an 'enemy of Islam' just three years earlier, but which had normalized relations with Rafsanjani's Iran by 1991.[15] Rafsanjani complemented these efforts through his critical but behind-the-scenes role in securing the release of some Western hostages held by Hezbollah in Lebanon.[16] When the United States launched and headed the 1990 military campaign to liberate Kuwait and punish Saddam in the Gulf War, Tehran adopted a rather muted stance. It created no obstacles to US military action against Iran's old foe, despite voicing vehement opposition to massive American military deployment in the Gulf.

Rafsanjani's overtures, however, failed to elicit any positive response from Washington, for two main reasons. First, the United States was keen to maintain its recently established military presence in the Persian Gulf, and felt that a rapprochement between Iran and the GCC members might undermine the US position in this respect. Second, the warming of US relations with many Arab states generated anxieties in Israel and prompted Tel Aviv to push for a harder US line against Iran. Israeli politicians and lobbyists urged Washington to make the containment of Iran a top priority, claiming that Iran was 'insane' and represented a nuclear threat to the region and the world.[17] The result was the US policy of 'dual containment' of Iran and Iraq during the first term of President Bill Clinton (1993–97).[18] The United States now treated both countries as enemies, with a determination to isolate them in the international system, to bring about regime change in each, to ratchet up international sanctions against them, and to play them off against one another whenever desirable so that they could check and weaken one another for the benefit of the United States and its allies. The wider aim of the policy was to divide the Persian Gulf states between adversaries (Iran and Iraq) and friends (GCC states), with the aim of ensuring that the latter would become increasingly dependent on the United States for security against what was presented as serious Iranian and Iraqi threats.[19]

Ultimately, the policy did not work, as both Tehran and Baghdad found ways to work around it. Denounced by several senior American political figures as illogical and ineffective,[20] the policy was quietly abandoned by the start of Clinton's second term. While this may have initially caused some relief among conciliatory forces in the United States and Iran, Washington's ongoing threats of regime change and military action, together with its deepening strategic ties to Saudi Arabia and its GCC partners, severely impeded opportunities for a tangible improvement in US–Iranian relations. Washington's policy behaviour lent credence in Iran to the *jihadis'* representation of the United States as bent on the destruction of the Islamic Republic. This dynamic severely constrained Rafsanjani's ability to press on with his objectives – even in the early 1990s – of economic liberalization and moderation in foreign policy.

Mohammad Khatami's 1997 landslide electoral victory on an *ijtihadi* platform, as discussed in chapter 3, opened yet another potential window for better Iran–US ties. In contrast to Rafsanjani, Khatami was a committed reformist who sought political *and* economic changes for Iranian society, while remaining within the scope of the Constitution. He called for a revision of Iran's foreign policy, based on the principles of 'dialogue between civilizations' and cross-cultural understandings within the international system of nation-states.[21] He promoted a new vision of Shi'a Islam that would be adaptive to changing times and conditions – a vision, Khatami claimed that Khomeini would have shared if he were alive.[22]

From the outset, Khatami signalled a strong desire for improved relations with the West, and especially the United States. In the aftermath of the events of 11 September 2001, his government cooperated with the United States on many issues, including the fight against al-Qaeda, the Taliban and Sunni extremism. As mentioned in chapter 3, this cooperation proved nowhere more critical than in the case of Afghanistan. Tehran not only helped the US with legitimizing its military intervention and set the trends in motion for a post-Taliban order in Afghanistan, but also pledged substantial financial assistance to the country's reconstruction at the January 2002 Tokyo Conference and subsequent relevant forums on Afghanistan.[23] In all this, Tehran's wider objective was to entice the United States to moderate its behaviour towards Iran for better relations.

83

However, the George W. Bush administration remained committed to a policy of containment vis-à-vis Iran and was especially eager to prevent the country from having influence in Afghanistan. This policy was largely based on a fear that the Iran-backed Afghan groups might undermine America's overall position in Afghanistan and the region. Washington therefore not only failed to respond positively to Tehran's gestures, but actually hardened its policy and attitude towards Iran. Khatami's hardline factional opponents, who viewed America's Afghan adventure as part of a wider attempt to tighten the noose around Iran, could not have been more satisfied. The United States' uncompromising posture provided them with a pretext for countering America's military presence in Afghanistan in whatever way possible, short of a direct military confrontation.

Khatami's efforts to shift Iranian foreign policy to a more reconciliatory posture thus faced serious obstacles as a result of both domestic and international factors. Washington justified its unresponsiveness to Khatami's overtures by maintaining that power did not rest with Khatami and his supporters, but rather with the *jihadi* factions. The escalation of US hostility to the Iranian Islamic regime in the aftermath of al-Qaeda's 11 September attacks on the United States and President Bush's declaration of the 'war on terror' was due partly to US suspicions that these factions in Iran may have been involved in the attacks. Hence Bush's condemnation of Iran as a member of an 'axis of evil', an accusation that aroused predictable outrage among Iranians.[24] Even after admitting that the CIA had found no evidence of a direct connection between Iran and al-Qaeda attacks (a finding confirmed in July 2004 by the 9/11 Commission Report), Bush insisted that he would continue to investigate the possibility of Iranian involvement.[25] By 2005, continued *jihadi* pressure on the Khatami government coupled with a lack of real Western goodwill, had taken their toll.

The nuclear issue

Four years into Bush's 'war on terror', the conservative camp re-emerged as the dominant cluster in the *Majles*, and Ahmadinejad, representing segments of the *jihadi* cluster, was elected to the presidency. A focal point of Ahmadinejad's electoral campaign had been Khatami's 'concessionary' foreign policy, which, according to the *jihadi* cluster, had aided Western powers while weakening Iran. Invoking Khomeini's emphasis on national self-sufficiency, Ahmadinejad opted for a confrontational foreign policy posture, aggressive language (particularly against Israel) and an emphasis on Iran's right to nuclear development, ensuring the nuclear issue became a salient one during his presidency.[26]

The history of Iran's nuclear programme dates back to the Shah's rule, when an initiative was launched with US support and participation.[27] Under the Shah, Iran ratified the Nuclear Non-Proliferation Treaty (NPT) in 1970. The Islamic Republic has remained both a signatory to the NPT and a member of the International Atomic Energy Agency (IAEA) since that time. Indeed, following the Iranian revolution, Khomeini declared nuclear weapons to be against the 'spirit of Islam' and Iran's nuclear programme was halted. However, after the war with Iraq and an assessment of Iran's future energy needs, the Islamic leadership found it once more desirable to develop Iran's nuclear facilities for peaceful purposes, and continued its efforts in this respect through the 1990s with Russian and Chinese assistance.

US and Israeli fears over the extent of the programme escalated following the discovery of two previously unknown nuclear reactors at Natanz and Arak in 2002. Although the IAEA concluded in 2004 that it had found no evidence of illegal activities on the part of the Iranians[28] – a finding that was later confirmed by US intelligence estimates in 2007 and 2012, which reported that Iran was not necessarily on track to produce an atomic bomb – Iran's nuclear programme continued to be met with immense hostility in the United States and Israel. In 2006, Iran had been referred to the UN Security Council for failure to meet safeguard requirements under the NPT. When Iran refused UN demands to stop its uranium enrichment, it was subjected to stringent economic sanctions. In defiance of these sanctions and calls for international dialogue, Ahmadinejad pressed forward with enrichment. However, in 2010, Tehran agreed to a nuclear swap deal, brokered by two mutually respected US-allied leaders, Brazilian President Lula da Silva and Turkish Prime Minister Recep Tayyip Erdogan. The deal, under which Iran would send to Turkey 1,200 kilograms of its enriched uranium to be turned into fuel for Iran's reactors, was the same deal that had been demanded in Iran's negotiations with three European powers – Britain, France and Germany. However, the United States rejected the deal on the grounds that it could not trust Tehran, thus squandering a unique opportunity to test Tehran's sincerity.

In 2011, during Ahmadinejad's second term, the IAEA produced a second report indicating the possibility that Iran was seeking to develop military nuclear capacities. Although the results were inconclusive, they contributed to the imposition of even tougher Western sanctions against Iran. In 2012, Iran was put under a joint US–European Union oil embargo and its banks were disconnected from SWIFT, the network used by the majority of the world's banks for international monetary transactions. This played a key part in a dramatic contraction of the Iranian economy, which contributed to mass unemployment and exacerbated inflation rates.

Rouhani's reformist agenda

Rouhani's electoral triumph came at a critical moment for the Iranian regime. After eight years of hardline conservatism under Ahmadinejad, Iran was in the grip of international isolation, political and social stagnation, and economic crisis, with rocketing inflation rates and plummeting oil revenues plaguing the nation and society at large. A contributing factor to this predicament was Iran's nuclear programme, which had emerged as the critical issue in US–Iranian relations. Rouhani was now placed to address a set of problems that had been building incrementally over a long period of time.

Rouhani came to power as a highly seasoned, experienced and deft *ijtihadi*-inclined clerical and political figure. A widely respected British-educated lawyer, academic, diplomat and political activist, he had been closely associated with the Islamic system, and operated within the *jihadi/ijtihadi* framework laid down by Ayatollah Khomeini from the early days of the Islamic Republic. He had risen through the ranks of the state apparatus, serving in a range of positions as a member of the Assembly of Experts, the Expediency Council and the Supreme National Security Council, of which he was also secretary from 1989 to 2005. Further, he had been an elected member of the *Majles* and Deputy Speaker of that body twice. He had served as an economic and trade negotiator, and as Iran's chief nuclear negotiator under Khatami. Meanwhile, he had headed the Center for Strategic Research – Iran's premier think-tank for influential policymakers – from 1992 until his election to the presidency, and authored several monographs with a focus on Iran's foreign relations and its place in world politics.[29] More importantly, he had maintained effective organizational ties with the Supreme Leader and good working relationships with all other factions in Iranian politics. As such, he was viewed as a loyal insider and interlocutor, capable of strengthening the regime by reconnecting it to its original popular base and improving its international standing.

Rouhani began his presidency on 2 August 2013. After assembling a cabinet composed predominantly of qualified technocrats, including the US-educated and experienced diplomat, Mohammad Javad Zarif, who was appointed foreign minister with the endorsement of the Supreme Leader and the conservative-dominated *Majles*, Rouhani identified four issues, which he had articulated during his election campaign, as his government's top priorities. They were: to improve social and economic living conditions for the Iranian people; to relax political and social controls and secure the release of political prisoners; to engage the West, and the United States in particular, for a settlement of the nuclear dispute, without compromising Iran's right to uranium enrichment for peaceful purposes; and to uphold the rights of ethnic and religious minorities and to initiate a 'civil rights charter'.

To stabilize the Iranian currency (rial) and the economy, Rouhani needed to engage in structural rather than cosmetic reforms involving tighter fiscal and monetary measures by reining in the money supply, which had ballooned and fuelled inflation under Ahmadinejad. He also needed to get rid of food and fuel subsidies, cut back public spending, expand the space for the private sector and reform the public service, streamlining bureaucratic procedures and changing relevant laws to reduce red tape. The last of these was particularly important in light of the need to attract substantial domestic and foreign investment, and facilitate wider and diversified trade with the outside world. Rouhani also needed to tackle inefficiency, patronage and corruption in the governmental system and beyond, devise an effective system of taxation, overhaul the Iranian oil industry, which was badly in need of technological renovation and financial investment, and generate political and social conditions conducive to individual initiative and creativity, with an emphasis on the promotion of political and civil liberties. In addition, it was imperative for Rouhani to curtail the activities and influence of forces that had a vested interest in the preservation of the existing system. These forces included the *Sepah*, the *Basij* and the *bonyads*. At the same time he also proved adept at tackling the conservative factions within the *Majles*, around the Supreme Leader and throughout the governmental system in ways that could enable him to implement his reforms. Yet, above all, it was also necessary for him to reach an accommodation with the United States and its European allies over Iran's nuclear programme in order to end sanctions, which could help him with his domestic reforms and open the way for a US-Iranian rapprochement.

By the end of his first year in office, Rouhani had initiated a number of promising measures in many of these areas. In regard to the economy, while the rial still remained very volatile and stagflation continued to be prominent, there were some signs of economic recovery. According to the International Monetary Fund estimates:

> The official inflation rate has come down to 32.5 percent from above 40 percent in mid-2013 ... gross domestic product [had been expected to] grow 1.5 percent [in 2014] after shrinking to 5.6 percent in 2012 and 1.7 percent in 2013 ... [g]rowth in projected budget spending for the current fiscal year [2014/15] was slowed to 9 percent.[30]

Rouhani also issued a 'civil rights charter' for discussion. The charter is far from being the most liberal document. It nonetheless provides a basis for reassuring national minorities – Arabs, Turks, Kurds, Baluchis and Bahais – and may therefore assist in the development of civil society as a foundation for robust political pluralism, while remaining within Khomeini's Islamic framework.

Rouhani concurrently launched a concerted diplomatic effort and so-called 'charm offensive' to secure a resolution of the nuclear issue, and to reassure Iran's Arab neighbours of his commitment to better relations and to a peaceful nuclear programme. He evidently did so with the solid backing of the Supreme Leader. Ali Khamenei, who has in the past echoed Khomeini's assertion that nuclear weapons are 'un-Islamic' and that Iran will not produce them, has reiterated this position in support of Rouhani's efforts.[31] This was with the clear caveat that Iran will not forego its right to develop its nuclear programme for non-military purposes and will not capitulate to the West when it comes to Iran's national and security interests. This was the first time that the Supreme Leader and the Iranian president had voiced a common position on the nuclear issue.

A US–Iranian thaw and motivating factors

To punch through more than three decades of profound distrust in US–Iranian relations, and a two-year deadlock in nuclear negotiations, Rouhani made a goodwill telephone call to President Barack Obama after attending the UN General Assembly meeting on 28 September 2013. This marked a milestone development – the first of its kind since the Iranian revolution. Rouhani entrusted Foreign Minister Zarif to resume nuclear negotiations with the Group of 5+1 (the five permanent members of the UN Security Council plus Germany) under the leadership of the High Representative of the European Union for Foreign Affairs and Security Policy, Baroness Catherine Ashton, who was succeeded by the former Polish prime minister, Donald Tusk, in August 2014. Meanwhile, one of Zarif's deputies, Abbas Araghchi, a figure from Ahmadinejad's era with reputedly good links to the Supreme Leadership, was tasked to assist the minister in the process. This soon led to direct negotiations between Zarif and his American counterpart, Secretary of State John Kerry, as another watershed event.

Rouhani made these moves not in a vacuum, but rather was enabled to do so by the mutually receptive actions of President Obama. The US leader had made a series of overtures towards the Iranian leadership for a peaceful resolution of the nuclear dispute and possible settlement of other differences during his presidential campaign and shortly after assuming office in 2009. As early as March of that year, in a Persian New Year (Nowruz) message sent directly to the government of 'the Islamic Republic of Iran' and to its people, Obama had called for 'engagement that is honest and grounded in mutual respect', and quoted from the thirteenth-century renowned Persian poet Sa'adi: 'The children of Adam are limbs of one body / Which God created from one essence.'[32] He reinforced this message in his June 2009 Cairo speech by calling for a 'new beginning' between the two sides, with expressions of a willingness 'to move forward without preconditions on the basis of mutual respect' and interest.[33] He was also the first US president to acknowledge America's role in the over-throw of Mossadeq's government in 1953 as part of US interference in Iranian politics and as an important factor in Iranian hostilities towards America. Although he never responded to Khamenei's 2008 demand for an apology, Obama and the CIA came very close to pub-licly expressing regret over the episode in 2012.

Obama also repeatedly cautioned Israel (more specifically its right-wing Prime Minister Benjamin Netanyahu) and the Jewish state's supporters within the US Congress against launching any unilateral military action against Iran that could jeopardize US diplomatic efforts. However, while Ahmadinejad was in power, no positive response materialized. Rouhani, on the other hand, could now capitalize on Obama's overtures in order to engage in proactive diplomacy in the context of changing conditions for both sides, with the factor of mutual need and vulnerability playing a key motivating role in the process.

Once the dominant geopolitical actor in the Middle East, the United States has experienced a dramatic decline in regional influence since the turn of the century. This is due not only to the 'loss' of Iran, but also to the United States' policy failures and mismanagement of a host of issues in the region. These have prominently included the wars in Iraq and Afghanistan, which have tarnished the United States' status as a formidable military power and political actor in the Middle East and beyond; the Israeli–Palestinian conflict, where the United States has been unable to pressure its strategic ally, Israel, into negotiating a lasting settlement with the Palestinians based on the principle of 'land for peace', which could result in the creation of an independent Palestinian state out of Israel's occupied territories on the 1967 borders; the Lebanese conundrum, where the United States has made no tangible progress in shifting the constellation of forces in favour of a stable and secure Lebanon; and the Syrian crisis, on the matter of which the United States has been paralysed, not knowing what to do to substantiate its opposition to Bashar al-Assad's rule.

Beyond these issues, the United States has been unable to deal effectively with the 'Arab Spring' or popular uprisings which started as pro-democracy revolts from late 2010 to early 2011 in Tunisia, Egypt, Libya, Yemen, Bahrain and Syria. Addressing these developments has been particularly difficult for the United States due to the fact that they pose a serious threat to America's oil-rich, conservative Arab allies, led by Saudi Arabia. The United States has been unable to deter Saudi Arabia and some of its GCC allies, especially the United Arab Emirates and Bahrain, from mounting a counter-revolution against pro-democratic and political Islamist forces in the Arab world. The role

93

played by these states has been critical in turning the Arab Spring into a winter of despair and soul-searching for pro-democracy elements that spearheaded the popular uprisings. This has been nowhere more evident than in Egypt, where the mid-2013 military overthrow of the democratically elected government of the Muslim Brotherhood, as ideologically monolithic and administratively incompetent as it may have been, set Egypt back on an authoritarian course of development. Washington has been instrumental in supporting this, despite its initial encouragement of pro-democracy forces in the country. Equally, the United States has failed to minimize the arena for al-Qaeda and its affiliates, as well as other extremist groups in the region.

The most recent of these groups is the Sunni Islamic State of Iraq and the Levant (*Al-Dawlah Al-Islamiyah fi Al-Iraq wa Al-Sham*, or ISIL), which by mid-2014 had succeeded in taking large swathes of territory in the Sunni-dominated western provinces of Iraq as well as northeastern Syria. The group declared an Islamic state (*khilafat* – caliphate) in its conquered territories and renamed itself simply Islamic State (IS) in June of the same year, issuing a call to all Muslims to join it under the single leadership of Abu Bakr al-Baghdadi, the self-proclaimed *Khalifa* (caliph) of all Muslims. IS's establishment of a '*khilafat*' has been almost universally rejected by governments and religious authorities alike, and subsidiary movements in the Muslim world and the group itself have been condemned as terrorist organizations which nonetheless remain a magnet for many radical Islamists (many of them arguably misguided and disenfranchised). The rise of IS is also a serious, existential challenge to Iraq and Syria, as well as to their neighbours, especially Iran, and further afield.

Given the array of forces – from Iran to the Gulf Arab states to the United States and Russia – opposed to it, IS's *khilafat* may not last in the long run. However, the fact that it has come into existence signals two things. The first is the magnitude of the power vacuum, which has occurred not only in Iraq and Syria, but also in the region. The second is that the radical forces of political Islam are here to stay for as long as popular causes exist. These causes range from Israel's brutal occupation of the Palestinian lands, most importantly including East Jerusalem, to a lack of political pluralism and wider participation and prevalence of socioeconomic disparities and injustices in the Arab/Muslim world, to a perception amongst Muslims of the United States and some of its allies as 'evil' (a perception fuelled by US military and political action, and its support of various authoritarian regimes in the region), as well as the deepening of Sunni–Shi'a divisions, on which the radical Muslim groups can draw to justify their extremist actions and widen their circle of jihadist recruitment. Ironically, IS's actions have already catapulted Syria and Iraq towards increased sectarian violence, bloodshed and disintegration – each of which is a factor that contributed to the emergence and success of IS in the first place.

With no coherent Middle East policy, the United States has vacillated in its support between a variety of contrasting forces, including democracy, authoritarianism, extremism, secularism and reformist Islamism, in order to maintain a new niche of influence for itself in the Middle East, with little or no success in recent times. On different levels, the United States' approach has proved to be contradictory and in some cases self-defeating. As a result, the United States has lost out to its adversaries, disappointed its friends and allies (Israel and Saudi Arabia in particular) and generated opportunities for Russia and China to seek greater roles vis-à-vis the United States in the region. Iran, ironically, has been the main beneficiary of US interventionist and policy debacles. US policy actions have markedly assisted Iran in building a strong regional position, with strong leverage in Afghanistan, Iraq, Syria and Lebanon.

US policy debacles and Iran's regional influence

In relation to Afghanistan, Tehran has capitalized on its substantial financial and reconstruction aid to the country, booming cross-border trade and economic and cultural ties with western Afghan provinces. It has also succeeded in developing close relations with a number of Afghan, particularly Shi'a, groups, whose followers form about 15–20 per cent of Afghanistan's population. Moreover, it has been able to forge close relations with some powerful government figures, including President Hamid Karzai (2001–14), who received substantial periodic Iranian cash payments for 'meeting the expenses of his office',[34] enabling Tehran to gain influence at the highest level of government in Afghanistan. Although the United States has from time to time made allegations that Iran has supplied arms to elements of the Taliban, such allegations fly in the face of the fact that Iran has been highly vigilant of the Pakistan-backed Taliban as a radical Sunni group, with a history of anti-Iranian activities. Equally, it is not in Iran's interest to see the return of Pakistan's influence in Afghanistan, as was the case when the Taliban were in power in Kabul (1996–2001).

While superficially, Iranian–Pakistani relations exhibit a degree of normalcy, serious tensions continue to underscore these relations. Tehran has long suspected Pakistan of supporting separatist groups such as *Jundullah* in the Baluchi-populated areas of southeastern Iran. More consequentially, it has remained wary of the US–Pakistan relationship and the deepening of strategic ties between nuclear-armed but volatile and cash-strapped Islamabad and an extremely wealthy, oil-rich Riyadh, wary of Iran's nuclear programme. Yet, the growing distrust between Karzai and his American counterpart and the fluctuating nature of the US–Pakistan 'patron–client' relationship (where Pakistan has often acted as both partner in, and manipulator of, the 'war on terror' to promote its interests in Afghanistan and the region), have provided Tehran with ample opportunities to circumvent America's efforts to limit Iranian influence in Afghanistan.

Similarly, Tehran has succeeded in building effective and wide-ranging leverage in Iraq. Tehran found it expedient to support the US overthrow of Saddam in 2003, but opposed its occupation of Iraq, suspecting that the Americans' real target was Iran. Tehran therefore adopted a two-pronged strategy in Iraq. On the one hand, it urged some of its powerful allies within the Iraqi Shi'a majority, who had been suppressed under Saddam's Sunni minority-dominated regime, to let the American push for democratization deliver power to them. On the other hand, whenever deemed necessary, it backed its Iraqi allies to ensure America remained entangled in a prolonged and bloody conflict in Iraq so as to prohibit Washington from taking any punitive measures against Iran. This strategy proved very effective in foiling any attempt by the United States to prevent the expansion of Iranian influence in Iraq. It helped the Shi'ites to score well in the 2005 elections, resulting in the establishment of a Shi'a-dominated government for the first time in Iraq's history as a modern state. On the other hand, it also contributed to the polarization of the three major Iraqi communities – the Shi'ites, the Sunnis and the Kurds – as the government became increasingly exclusionary in its attitude towards the Sunnis, and as the Kurds succeeded in almost setting up a state of their own in the north. By the time the US forces left Iraq at the end of 2011, Iraq was still highly volatile, but Tehran managed to have some powerful proxy forces in the country.[35]

Prominent among Tehran's Iraqi allies was the firebrand cleric Muqtada al-Sadr and his Mahdi Army, which has largely been trained and armed by Iran. Iran also sustained connections with Prime Minister Nur al-Maliki's *Da'wa* group and its allied parties, as well as Ammar al-Hakim and his Islamic Supreme Council of Iraq. Further, Tehran had extensive involvement in Iraqi security training, and numerous cultural and reconstruction projects. By all accounts, Iran has had far more influence in Baghdad in the wake of the US withdrawal than the United States itself. Iran's strategic partnership with Assad's Shi'a-linked minority Alawite regime in Syria also became central to the country's regional interests and security architecture. Tehran has therefore done whatever possible to provide the Syrian regime with all-round support to ensure its survival in the face of a nationwide but highly divided Sunni-dominated opposition since early 2011. In addition, the Assad regime has served as a centrepiece in bridging Iran's relations with Hezbollah in Lebanon. Tehran has viewed its sectarian and strategic relations with all Afghan, Iraqi, Syrian and Lebanese forces as critical to its regional security interests, especially in light of the ongoing enmity between Iran and Israel.

However, this does not mean that Iran has gained regional supremacy. Its position continues to be challenged by numerous governmental and subnational forces. At the governmental level, Saudi Arabia and several of its GCC partners – the United Arab Emirates, Kuwait and Bahrain in particular – have remained very watchful and deeply concerned about Iran's regional postures and nuclear programme. At the subnational level, Tehran's regional influence has been seriously challenged by such Sunni groups as IS in Iraq and Syria, al-Nusra in the latter, the Sunni opposition in Lebanon and the Taliban and their supporters in Afghanistan. Even so, Tehran has managed to defy regional and Western pressure and has built what may be called an Iran-centred strategic entity, stretching from Afghanistan to Lebanon. It has also been able to circumvent, to a noticeable degree, the effects of harsh Western sanctions, by widening its trade, economic and security ties on a barter basis with Eastern powers and using indirect means and ways to get around the sanctions as much as possible.

Contiguous with this development, Iran has fostered a very cooperative relationship with Russia, which has become an important trading partner and supplier of military hardware and nuclear technology to Iran. While there are no reliable figures available for Iranian purchases of Russian weapons, Russo-Iranian trade amounted to a total of about US$4 billion in 2012.[36] The two sides have cooperated closely in the field of nuclear technology since the early 1990s. For instance, Russia built a 1,000 megawatt light-water nuclear power plant in Bushehr, where some 3,500 Russian technicians have reportedly been employed.

Moscow has increasingly found the Iranian and Syrian regimes, and even their regional proxies, important in its strategy to secure a counter-US niche of influence in the Middle East. This strategy has gained greater potency in light of its souring relations with the United States and its allies over alleged Russian interference in eastern Ukraine, the subsequent imposition of Western economic sanctions on Russia and the latter's retaliatory measures since mid-2014.

Iran's economic and trade relations have grown even more extensively with China. The value of trade between the two countries reached close to US$40 billion in 2013. By 2014, China was also importing some 11 per cent of its annual oil needs from Iran.[37] Between 2005 and 2012, Iran was the sixth largest recipient (the largest recipient in the Middle East) of Chinese non-bond investment, which amounted to US$6.8 billion. China has grown to be Iran's largest trading partner, with around 70 Chinese companies involved in various fields and activities in Iran, including building bridges, tunnels and a subway system in Tehran. The Iranian markets are now flooded with Chinese goods. Chinese officials, technicians and traders form the bulk of regular foreign visitors to Iran – something which was once the province of the Americans.

Similarly, Indo-Iranian commercial ties have grown over the years. India imports on average some 16 per cent of its annual oil consumption from Iran. In return, since the imposition of sanctions, Iran receives a proportion of its oil revenue in Indian goods and services and a proportion in rupees.[38] Although the Indian purchase of Iranian oil declined by a noticeable percentage in 2013, it picked up again in 2014. The number of Indian companies and businesses engaged in different economic and industrial projects has seen steady growth.

Irrespective of its domestic problems and foreign policy complications with the West and the Gulf Arab states, Iran has reasserted itself as a key player in the region. It has acquired the necessary capacity to act as a regional stabilizer or destabilizer. As such, it is in a position to help the United States to leave a relatively stable Afghanistan behind, and to play constructive roles in Iraq (where Iranian and American interests against IS now coincide), Syria and Lebanon. In the event of a restoration of US–Iranian relations, Iran could substantially assist Washington to reconfigure its regional presence and influence – not as the dominant geopolitical actor, but as an important one capable of working sensitively and prudently within a paradigm of reconciling American interests with those of regional countries for regional stability and security.

At the same time, Iran could benefit greatly from US assistance. Given Rouhani's earnest need to fulfil his reformist agenda, it has been of paramount importance that he is able to bring an end to the sanctions and to open Iran up to wider economic and trade dealings with the West. Iran needs foreign investment and high technology to overhaul its oil industry and improve the living conditions for a majority of its people, who have been suffering for too long from stagnation on multiple fronts. The sooner the sanctions are lifted, the quicker Rouhani and his government will be in a position to take greater steps in fulfilling their promises to the Iranian people.

An interim nuclear agreement

It was in this context that the Rouhani government signed an interim agreement on Iran's nuclear programme with the Group of 5+1 on 24 November 2013. The agreement was to be implemented within six months from 1 January 2014. Under the deal, while claiming to have retained its right to uranium enrichment (as provided by the NPT) and to the continuation of activities in its nuclear sites in the cities of Arak, Fordo and Natanz, Iran undertook to freeze its uranium enrichment at a level of 5 per cent. It also agreed 'to neutralize its existing stockpile of near-20 per cent uranium' by diluting it to below 5 per cent.[39] Further, it committed itself to allowing more international inspections of its nuclear facilities. In return, the Western powers suspended some of the sanctions, enabling Iran to have access to US$7 billion in foreign exchange, as well as pledging not to impose additional sanctions, unless Iran failed to meet its commitment and reach a comprehensive agreement before the expiry of the interim deal on 20 July 2014. The interim agreement, which was achieved within a short space of time (to the surprise of many), was significant, as it marked an unprecedented thaw in US–Iranian relations. As both sides acknowledged, it was an initial step in a long and arduous process of negotiation that lay ahead before a comprehensive deal could be struck. After the IAEA had verified that Iran had met its end of the bargain, a round of negotiations for a comprehensive agreement took place in May 2014. However, these negotiations ended without a definitive outcome. Despite Iranian Foreign Minister Zarif's optimism that an agreement was possible in the next round of negotiations, the two sides still appeared to remain wide apart.

As a result, despite the noticeable headway that the two sides made in the negotiations, they could not overcome their differences to the extent necessary to meet the 20 July 2014 deadline. This meant that more time was needed before a comprehensive settlement could be reached. The United States and its partners agreed to a four-month extension. During this period, the Iranian side agreed to 'convert a portion of its 20 per cent uranium in powdered form to fuel plates for the Tehran Research Reactor, making it even less easily accessible for use in a weapons programme', and the West undertook to suspend some secondary sanctions and release a small amount of Iran's oil revenue held overseas, to the sum of US$2.8 billion.[40] Although there was no guarantee that a final agreement would be concluded by the end of the extension, the two sides appeared at least to have built some mutual trust and confidence, with a belief that the final goal was achievable.

Sources of opposition

During the process of negotiations, there was always the danger of derailment. Both sides faced stringent domestic and regional forces that viewed and continue to do so any kind of normalization of relations as against their vested interests. Although backed by the Supreme Leader, Rouhani had to work his way through a minefield of opposition from hardliners in his dealings with the United States. He has strong opponents within and outside the clerical elite. From within the clerical ranks, two of his most influential critics are Ayatollah Mesbh Yazdi and Ayatollah Ahmad Jannati. Yazdi is a former student of Ayatollah Khomeini, a member of the Council of Experts since 1990 and also director of the Imam Khomeini Education and Research Institute and a staunch supporter of Khamenei. Ahmadinejad was and continues to be a strong follower of Yazdi. Jannati is secretary of the powerful Council of Guardians and, like Yazdi, is a devotee of Khomeini and supporter of Khamenei. Both ayatollahs have opposed any concessions to the West and Jannati has not hesitated to advocate war with the US and Israel, if required in defence of the Islamic regime and Iran.

Outside the clerical circle, apart from Ahmadinejad, opposition to Rouhani is spearheaded by the old-hand conservative Hossein Shariatmadari, director and editor-in-chief of the government-owned *Kayhan* newspaper. He is close to Khamenei, with whom he reportedly meets regularly on a weekly basis, and a strong supporter of Ahmadinejad. In the wake of the disputed 2009 elections, he called for the trial of the reformist leaders and intimated threateningly that Khatami could be assassinated. In addition, the *jihadi* opponents of Rouhani have a strong presence in the Revolutionary Guard, the *Basij*, the *Majles*,[41] and the governmental system overall, and include several of Ahmadinejad's former ministers, especially his minister of petroleum, Massoud Mir Kazami. These figures and many more like them still have not come to terms with Rouhani's approach and the country's patent need for better relations with the United States. Their continued opposition to the United States is an important strategy for maintaining their ideological stance, political and economic power and religious influence in the polity. In moving towards a comprehensive nuclear agreement with the Group of 5+1, Rouhani had no choice but to take his factional opponents' concerns on board. The agreement had to be one that could satisfy his supporters and opponents equally.

President Obama has found himself in a similar situation. He, too, has faced vehement opposition in his dealings with Iran from the forces of the right.

The ultraconservative Tea Party movement, backed by conservative think-tanks and media outlets, has led the pack in this respect. These groups have relentlessly painted the Iranian Islamic regime as brutally fundamentalist and unyieldingly theocratic, and have invoked the memory of the hostage crisis of 35 years ago to remind the president and the American public of the dangers of dealing with Iran. Although a minority, they have a strong voice within and outside Congress, and are keen to reap whatever political and ideological kudos they can from opposing any process towards the normalization of US relations with Iran. This means that the final nuclear agreement and its ensuing developments had to be of a nature that would enable Obama to sell it to his domestic critics as well.

The problems do not stop at the domestic level. There has also been strong regional opposition to any serious opening in US–Iranian relations. Israel has remained adamantly opposed to any kind of nuclear agreement as well as to restoration of normal relations between the United States and Iran. Prime Minister Netanyahu and his supporters in Israel and the American Congress, who in a way mirror the Iranian hardliners, have totally focused on Iran as an existential threat. Whilst US Secretary of State Kerry and his European counterparts described the November 2013 interim nuclear agreement with Iran as a historic event, Netanyahu condemned it as a 'historical mistake' and warned the Obama administration against making any concessions to Tehran.[42] He has persistently invoked the threat of Israel's use of military force against Iran, despite the fact that he has repeatedly been told by several former and current high-ranking Israeli security figures that Iran is neither about to produce nuclear weapons, nor does it intend to do so. The Obama administration has tried to counter Netanyahu's bellicose stance through a policy of reassurance and discreet pressure in order to increase the possibilities for diplomacy.

Ironically, the position of the Israelis and the American right is shared by Saudi Arabia and some of its GCC partners. In fact, the fear of Iran is so great in Riyadh, Abu Dhabi and Kuwait City that Iran is now viewed as more of an enemy than Israel. Former Saudi King Abdullah called on the Americans to cut down Iran like the 'head of a snake',[43] and there have even been reports that the Saudis would be willing to let Israelis use their air space for an attack on Iran. Iran has been described by a leading Saudi figure, Prince Turki al-Faisal, as a 'paper tiger with steel claws'.[44] Yet, no hard evidence has been produced to substantiate the fear that dominates the thinking and behaviour of many Gulf Arab states towards Iran. Tehran's strategic relations with Syria, its close sectarian and material ties with certain Iraqi Shi'a groups, its sectarian and political support for the majority Shi'a population of Bahrain against the minority Sunni-dominated government, and its links with Hezbollah, which the GCC states denounced as a terrorist organization in 2013, are often cited as evidence for the Arab states of the Persian Gulf's deep suspicions towards Iran. No consideration seems to be given to the fact that Iran's gains on those fronts have been mainly due to US policy fiascos and, ironically, Saudi Arabia's support, at least until recently, of various Sunni extremist groups, whether in Iraq or Syria or Lebanon or Bahrain. Given the challenges facing Iran even in those countries where it has made some gains, and its own dire economic situation, Tehran is not realistically positioned to become seriously adversarial towards the Gulf Arab states.

Relations between the Islamic Republic of Iran and the United States have been historically very turbulent and costly for both sides. With the advent of Rouhani's government, a window of opportunity opened. The two sides made use of it in order to work their way through more than three decades of distrust and hostility. A failure on the part of Rouhani to achieve some of his main policy goals would once again strengthen his factional opponents' hardline attitude towards the United States and its allies, most importantly Israel, as happened to his predecessors Presidents Rafsanjani and, more importantly, Khatami, resulting in the excesses of the Ahmadinejad administration. The United States, for its part, would remain deprived of cooperation from the very actor that could be of the most significant assistance to it in the region. Iran needs US help to overcome its isolation and social and economic problems and the United States requires Iran's assistance to play a more effective and constructive role in improving its standing and helping resolve some of the tragic conflicts in the region. They are both in need of, and vulnerable to, one another. This constitutes enough of a motivation to bring the two sides together to discover common ground for better relations, provided the detractors are not allowed to prevent them from moving forward. Neutralizing these detractors, both domestic and regional, is a challenge that both sides will have to overcome.

5

The Complex Road Ahead

The future of the Islamic Republic of Iran may prove to be as complicated as the journey that it has travelled so far. Iran's religious political order – and the foreign policy it has pursued to maintain and strengthen this order in a highly volatile and contested region – are set to shape the country's future, both on the home front and on the global stage. Despite President Hassan Rouhani's efforts to chart a moderate, reformist Islamist course of change and development for his country, the tension, conflict and fragmentation which have beset Iran since Ayatollah Ruhollah Khomeini's death in 1989 continue to feature in the political life of the nation's ruling elite. Divisions at the top, together with the nature of the governmental system operating under it, have produced disruptive governance, economic mismanagement and sociocultural malaise, with serious consequences for the state and society at large. Economic stagnation, involving unacceptable levels of unemployment and inflation, as well as a lack of critical livelihood resources, have posed a problem for many Iranians on a day-to-day basis. Human rights violations and the stymie of dissent have affected Iranians and their families. The growing dichotomy between state and society and the politics of fear and distrust – both within the government and amongst the public – have eroded the confidence of many Iranian peoples in their country's religio-political order. This has spawned a situation where people cannot trust people and self-censorship is common.

The Islamic Republic's domestic difficulties cannot be considered in isolation from the regional and international contexts in which they have emerged. Indeed, these difficulties have been closely tied to Iran's external relations, particularly to its relationship with the United States. The interplay between the Islamic government's domestic politics and foreign policy circumstances has played a critical role in shaping Iran today, and will be crucial in determining its future direction.

This chapter assesses Iran's future in light of its historical experiences and the shifting regional and international contexts. While there is no shortage of ways in which this topic might be examined, the chapter offers an analysis of Iran's prospects in light of four paramount and closely connected issues of historical and contemporary significance for the Islamic Republic. The issues are: the incongruity within Iran's Islamic system of governance; the country's structural economic problems; Iran's relations with the United States and its key European allies; and the complexity and unpredictability of the changing regional situation.

Incongruity in governance

As we have seen, the divisions that long lurked beneath the surface of Iran's political scene have, from the early 2000s, become increasingly impossible to conceal. The public outcry and violent government crackdown that followed the controversial re-election of Mahmoud Ahmadinejad in 2009 brought to a bloody climax the longstanding schism between the *jihadi* and *ijtihadi* factions within the governing elite. This episode raised serious questions about Iran's two-tiered system of Islamic governance, as defined by the clerically appointed *velayat-e faqih* and the universally elected positions of the presidency and *Majles*. For the first time these questions were about not only the long-term viability of this system but also its short-term survivability when it was so disengaged from the Iranian people. On the one hand, and to the surprise of many, the Islamic Republic owes its longevity to the complexity of its two-tier governmental structure, which has provided Iranian politics with a degree of internal elasticity and external flexibility in response to changing threats and challenges. At the same time, with the passage of time, the two tiers have grown quite incongruous. The 2009 eruption of the schism between the *jihadi* and *ijtihadi* factions signalled a serious breakdown in Khomeini's vision for a political system made up of two tiers working organically, if unequally, with one another. The episode not only gave voice to the widespread disenchantment of the Iranian people with the political system, but also raised the question of whether, and for how long, such a divided system could remain in place.

More than bringing the conflicts between the *jihadi* and *itjtihadi* factions to a head, the events saw the divisions within each faction degenerate into open confrontation and rivalry. For example, the differences between Ali Khamenei and Ahmadinejad grew so tense that, in 2011, the Supreme Leader reportedly contemplated abolishing the presidency altogether. Although

The Complex Road Ahead

Khamenei's power and authority prevailed and a looming governing crisis was avoided, the underlying reasons for the tension arising from opposing lines of divinely sanctioned and popularly based authorities in the system, alongside the existing divisions between *jihadi* and *ijtihadi* factions, remained unresolved. Meanwhile, the Supreme Leader himself has not been immune from these issues. While Khamenei was able to rely on Khomeini's legacy of almost monolithic leadership to expand his control over all instruments of state power and eclipse the popular tier of government without fear of overt reproach, the degree of political plurality embedded in the Islamic order has meant that he is not invulnerable to criticism from reformists, including – and often especially and most bitingly – from its clerical elements.

Yet while all these divisions pose questions about the long-term viability of the Islamic Republic, they do not mean that the Islamic government now faces the threat of implosion or danger of a serious societal challenge. To the contrary, the regime is as secure as it can be. It has succeeded in silencing or marginalizing any fundamentally threatening form of opposition from within and outside the clerical ranks. The forces that may be capable of challenging the regime, such as the Islamic Revolutionary Guard Corps (IRGC), which is touted by some outside observers and analysts as the one with the greatest capacity to take over the government, do not find it in their interests to rock a system that serves them, and in whose construction and preservation they have played a key role. There is no sign of an effective threat from the secular liberal opposition either, and the same applies even more to the supporters of the late Shah, now led by his son, Mohammad Reza, from exile.

111

Nonetheless, the two-tier system has undeniably become problematic for Iran and confusing for the outside world, where governments and officials have often not been able work out with whom they should conduct business for a decisive outcome. The Supreme Leader, for instance, is widely recognized as the most powerful, but not the most easily accessible, political figure within Iran. The president, on the other hand, has proved to be more politically and diplomatically available, but he remains unable to deal with domestic and foreign policy issues decisively without the support of the Supreme Leader and his entourage. The issue gains wider complexity when considered in the context of the patronage networks, malpractices, bottlenecks and other varieties of dysfunctionality that the system hides within.

An obvious resolution to the problem is to streamline the two tiers and thus generate a single line of authority within a publicly mandated pluralist political system. However, the entrenched factional interests in the country present an immediate and obstinate barrier to such restructuring. Any attempt to weaken the overarching power of the Supreme Leader and to implement a fully workable pluralist system of governance under a popularly mandated single leadership is almost certain to be resisted not only by a handful of high-ranking, hard-minded clerics, but by the millions of ordinary Iranians who derive their privileges, and indeed livelihoods, from the current power system.

As a veteran insider, Rouhani is undoubtedly aware of the problems associated with the two-tier system. He knows how the divine-based tier has enabled the *jihadi* or hardline factions to ensconce themselves in a position of power, enabling them to frustrate the work of the reformist and pragmatist elements within and outside the organs of government whenever expedient. Rouhani was also witness to the ways in which such factions undermined Mohammad Khatami's reformist agenda and prevented him from achieving no more than what was needed to defuse the tensions within Iranian society and politics.

At the same time, Rouhani is a visionary, with a pragmatic agenda, a wide social platform, ample expertise and a commitment to good governance. He seems keen to take stock of Iran's domestic fragility and political discord as well as the country's progress beyond its hard revolutionary days in an attempt to set a moderate and reformist Islamic course for the nation. He evidently wants to see an Iran with a stable and dynamic political order, consisting of interactive and vibrant linkages between state and society within a pluralist Islamic framework. He appears to consider the realization of this vision essential for enabling Iran to assume the respect and international pre-eminence that the country deserves and which runs deeply in the Iranian collective political psyche. For this, Rouhani will need to overcome a number of observable obstacles at different levels.

Before discussing these obstacles, it is important to remember that despite his pragmatist zeal, Rouhani is himself a product of the system. As such, he cannot be expected to restructure the system, but rather to improve it by smoothing out some of its rough edges in pursuit of revitalizing its bases of public support and making it more functional, effective and viable, while enhancing its wider acceptability in the international arena – something that was significantly undermined under Ahmadinejad. In other words, Rouhani is keen to see the system work better without rocking its foundations. The reforms that he has so far advocated and unleashed are largely directed towards achieving this end. Moreover, the extent to which he will be able to succeed in realizing his reforms during his first (and possibly second) term in office will depend on the degree to which he can avoid impinging upon the authority and interests of the Supreme Leader and his cohorts, as well as their affiliated groups, who are deeply invested in the status quo.

Rouhani's presidency, therefore, brings to light a central paradox, which lies at the heart of the question of reform in the Islamic Republic. On the one hand, the turbulent birth of the Islamic government and the hostile international climate in which it has evolved have ensured the dominance of *jihadi* elements within the instruments and institutions of state power. For this reason, any attempt to reform the system has to contend with the factions whose chief interest lies in the perpetuation of that very system. On the other hand, the dysfunction and malpractice that this variable has generated have reached a point where they have threatened the legitimacy or even the viability of the Islamic government itself.

From one perspective, Rouhani is extremely well positioned to manoeuvre within these constraints in pursuit of reform. His credentials and experience within conservative branches of the Islamic government have arguably enabled him to enjoy more support from the Supreme Leader than any of his reformist predecessors. Yet, while Khamenei has backed Rouhani in his efforts to move forward on the intertwined issues of economic reform, resolution of the nuclear impasse and ending sanctions, he has concurrently ensured that he remains the final arbiter on any major domestic or foreign policy matters. He continues to distrust the United States and has repeatedly cautioned Rouhani and Mohammad Javad Zarif against stepping too far over the line. Khamenei's expressions of support for a deal with Washington on the nuclear issue have always been tempered by cautioning against any policy action or agreement that could possibly compromise Iran's national pride or impinge upon its Islamic order and standing as a fully independent Islamic state. This has meant that no matter what, Iran must be able to maintain its Shi'a Islamic identity and governance system, its course of development, as well as, more concretely, retain its right to enrich uranium for peaceful purposes.

Rouhani has already had some considerable setbacks at the hands of his hardline opponents in different arenas. This has noticeably complicated the relationship between the Supreme Leader and his devotees, and between Rouhani and his supporters on various domestic and foreign policy issues. For example, the Islamic regime has marked the last Friday of Ramadan (the Islamic fasting month) every year as the Qods or Jerusalem Day since 1979. On this occasion public rallies are held throughout Iran in solidarity with the Palestinian people and to denounce the occupation of the Palestinian lands as well as America's support for Israel. The Islamic Republic's leaders address the rallies, with many of them strongly condemning Israel as an aggressive and illegitimate state, and America as an imperialist power. In 2013, Rouhani addressed the Friday prayer gathering on that day and condemned Israel as 'a wound on the body of the Islamic world'.[1]

However, in 2014 he found it expedient to be more measured in marking the day. While in the midst of nuclear negotiations with the Group of 5+1, and needing to tone down Tehran's usual anti-Israeli and anti-American rhetoric of 'death to Israel' and 'death to America', Rouhani called for the demolition of the

Zionist regime 'by a referendum' and unconditional restoration of the rights of the Palestinians. Yet, he did not personally participate in the Friday prayer rally, leading to vehement and politically damaging reactions from his opponents, who accused him of selling out to the Americans and Israelis.[2] In a further blow to the president, on 20 August 2014 the *Majles* dismissed Rouhani's reformist Minister of Science, Reza Faraji Dana, for nominating four senior department officials from among those who had taken part in the opposition against Ahmadinejad in the 2009 elections, and who had allowed students to return to university after having been expelled 'for moral and political reasons'.[3] A strong anti-Rouhani bloc is well entrenched in the *Majles*, with the ability to scupper any of his legislative proposals with which it doesn't agree.

Complicating Rouhani's position further is the existence of many powerful extra-political organizations, such as the IRGC and the *Basij*, as well as the *bonyads*, whose loyalties lie firmly with the conservative causes, strongly follow the Supreme Leader and have immense political, social and economic resources at their disposal. A relaxation of Iran's political climate and ensuring that its system of governance works will require Rouhani to modify the system substantially, and for this he needs to persuade his conservative opponents and their supporting organizations to back him – even where this may appear to be against their particular economic self-interest.

Ultimately, the extent to which Rouhani may succeed or fail in reforming the political system will be critical to the future of the Islamic Republic and the direction that Iran takes. The task of aligning the two tiers of the system constitutes a serious challenge to Rouhani and his pragmatist and reformist supporters. So far, while being frequently vocal about the necessity for economic and social reforms, Rouhani has remained relatively muted in relation to the need for reform of the political system. He had initially promised political relaxation, including securing the freedom of political prisoners. But he did not find that an easy task. As of the start of 2015, figures like Mir-Hossein Mousavi and Mehdi Karoubi were still under house arrest, and the jails – or what the Iranian authorities have named 'corrective centres' – remained heavily populated by political prisoners. Nor have all arbitrary arrests and persecution for perceived political or moral differences stopped. The anomalous relationship between the Iranian state and society that persists is irreconcilable, and contains too many gridlocks for the Islamic Republic to realize an ideal and effective model to benefit the majority of its own citizens or outside actors in the Muslim world.

Economic gridlock

The economy is the second area that will determine Iran's future direction, and it, too, is a sector where fundamental reform is desperately needed. Rouhani has inherited an entrenched, oil-based rentier economy, largely controlled by the clerical elite and its subsidiaries. As with the political system, the corruption and dysfunction within the Iranian economy are at once a legacy of and a contributor to the Islamic Republic's controversial status in international relations. Sanctions and military conflicts have played an important part not only in stalling growth and discouraging investment, but also in fuelling corruption, poor administrative and bureaucratic practices, and

117

patronage politics within the rentier state. The lack of any clear conception of what 'Islamic economics' might look like has also contributed to the rise of an ineffective state economic structure, the monopolization of resources by elements of the ruling stratum and the gross mismanagement of state industries. Even if Rouhani manages to persuade or outmanoeuvre his factional opponents at the level of politics and ideology, reforming the economy and improving the public sector's efficiency constitutes a formidable challenge at the level of implementation. Nevertheless, Rouhani's success or failure in this area is bound to have a profound effect not only on the fortunes of the forces of moderation and reform in Iran, but also on the Islamic Republic as a whole in relation to its internal and external settings.

The historical and political contexts that have shaped the Islamic Republic's economic policies are key to understanding both the current state of affairs and the prospects for improvement in the future. During his lifetime, Khomeini emphasized the need to develop an 'Islamic' economic path, distinct from both capitalist and communist approaches. However, he provided few details on how this might be achieved; indeed, the valorization of the poor and downtrodden (*mostakhbarin*) in Khomeini's revolutionary Islamic discourse stood in tension with an economic policy geared towards growth and wealth creation.[4] Even Iran's first Islamic President Abol-Hassan Bani-Sadr, who had worked on the issue for years, could not come up with anything practical and workable in an increasingly sophisticated world economic environment.

The economy of the infant Islamic Republic was also seriously affected by the rapid outflow of human capital – in the form of seasoned managers, skilled workers, foreign technicians and other professionals – in the aftermath of the revolution. This was followed by the devastating war with Iraq, post-revolutionary turmoil and Islamic ideological orthodoxy, US sanctions and international isolation. Although Iran emerged from the war with no foreign debt, the human and material losses from the war and sanctions took a heavy and long-lasting toll on the Iranian people. The subsequent acceleration and widening of these sanctions only drove the dagger deeper into the country's economic health.

While detrimental in and of themselves, these developments were complemented by the mismanagement of the economy and state resources due to poor planning, inefficient administration and pervasive corruption, especially under Ahmadinejad. The presence of existential threats and economic exigencies in the formative years of the Islamic Republic provided the justification for the *jihadis'* consolidation of power and, with it, the monopolization of state resources. The mushrooming of *bonyads* as an instrument of financial and economic activities in support of state policies can be taken as exemplary. The *bonyads*, along with the *waqf* institution and other religious establishments, remain a cornerstone of conservative power in Iran, providing a substantial source of financial support for conservative elements that is unavailable to reformists.[5] Needless to say, the entrenched connection between economic privilege and factional political interests has not been conducive to sound processes of economic development.[6]

Yet if much of Iran's wealth is under the control of the clerical elite, largely through the system of *bonyads*,[7] some 70 per cent of the country's economy is currently tied up in the hands of the government

119

and state-affiliated enterprises or IRGC economic expansionism.[8] Moreover, much of what is a highly underdeveloped private sector is owned and controlled by well-placed individuals and families within the power structure or closely linked to it. The fortunes of the *bazaaris* (traditional marketplace merchants and businesses), who have historically formed the backbone of the Iranian economy, have increasingly become interconnected with members of the ruling stratum, blurring the distinction between the public and private sectors. Whatever the nature of the private sector, it is caught up in as much red tape and bureaucratic inefficiencies as government operations.

The nature of economic difficulties in contemporary Iran cannot be understood without reference to its longstanding status as a rentier state. As was the case under the Shah, the economy of the Islamic Republic is mostly oil-based, with revenue from oil and gas resources forming , directly and indirectly, some 70 per cent of the state's income and expenditure. Iran's oil exports stood at around 60 per cent of the country's gross domestic product (GDP) in 2011/12, fuelling violent price fluctuations and worsening the effects of Western sanctions.[9] The decline in the country's oil production from 4 million to 2.6 million barrels a day between 2009 and 2013 has taken a heavy toll on the government's income.[10] Government oil revenues experienced an even sharper decline in 2014, as crude prices dropped by about 40 per cent between June and December, with more decline to come at least in the short run, due largely to world overproduction and slow demand. During this period the price of Iranian crude oil fell from US$110 to less than US$70 per barrel and even lower in 2015.[11] A price of US$131 per barrel is required for Iran to balance its budget.

State control of the oil industry has exacerbated these issues, resulting in growing inefficiency and, as a consequence, lower profit margins. Iran's state-run oil industry was producing 70 per cent less in 2005 than in 1979, although it employed 126,000 more workers.[12] Oil-rentierism, along with its economic and political vicissitudes, has been a constant factor throughout Iran's modern history.

The ways in which the Islamic Republic has spent its fluctuating flows of petro-dollars gives further cause to reflect on the connection between the state's economic policy and its international status. For instance, national security is given top priority and substantial resources have been invested in the development of armament and related industries, with very high costs for the civilian sector. In 2013, of a GDP of US$429 billion and a budget of US$312 billion, Iran's direct military expenditure was reportedly US$17.7 billion. However, this figure did not include indirect expenditure on research and development of weapon systems and military aid to regional allies, which amounted to many more billions of dollars.[13] The 2013 direct military expenditure marked a decline from US$25.2 billion in the previous year, but in early 2014, Rouhani announced a rise of 33.5 per cent in the defence budget for fiscal year 2015/16. As such, military expenditure continues to consume a substantial chunk of the annual national revenue and budget.[14] The prioritization of defence in the Islamic Republic's budget reflects the continuing relevance of threat perception in economic decision-making.

Meanwhile, foreign investment remains very low in the country due in part to sanctions and in part to concerns about risk and return. The Islamic Republic has stepped up efforts to encourage foreign investors in recent years, and the country's official news agency has reported more than a twofold increase in foreign investment, from US$7.5 to US$16 billion, from 2013 to 2014 alone.[15] Yet Iran needs a lot more than this. Rouhani has called for increased foreign investment, including in the construction of Iran's railroads; he has criticized big 'monopolies' in Iran, amounting to an indirect challenge to the *Sepah*'s expanded involvement in the Iranian economy.[16] Nevertheless, national production has fallen short of meeting the expanding national consumption of a rapidly growing population. The Iranian industrial output (apart from traditional handicrafts, such as carpets), is not of a volume or quality to be competitive in the international market or to supersede Iran's domestically consumed agricultural and husbandry yields. Even the latter is heavily supplemented by imports of basic commodities, such as wheat, meat and dairy products, to meet national needs. For instance, while agriculture accounts for 92 per cent of Iran's water use, it produces enough food for only 66 per cent of the population; the rest has to be imported.[17] This is despite the fact that food self-sufficiency has remained a centrepiece of the Islamic Republic's rhetoric on economic policy since its inception.[18]

A great deal of investment has been made in infrastructural development, and Iran is today endowed with good all-season road and railway networks, ports and hydroelectric plants. There is also an expanding construction industry, which contributes noticeably to the economy. However, like most other economic activities, these sectors are dominated by government or government-linked companies and enterprises, and are blotted with corrupt and inefficient practices. Corruption has become so endemic that it permeates every sector at all levels. According to Transparency

International, Iran ranked 144th in the world in terms of corruption perceptions in 2013.[19]

As the country has remained largely closed to outsiders, it is only in recent years that the authorities have relaxed entry visa requirements to some extent. The tourism industry remains in its infancy. For it to become a bourgeoning revenue-earning sector and therefore a main contributor to national economic activities, Tehran needs not only to soften its distrust of foreigners, but also to build a lot more tourism facilities than it currently possesses. This is where the private sector and foreign investment can play a key role, given the right political and economic environment.

Iran also has a very inefficient taxation system, which has grown expeditiously on the premise of more political/ideological expediency rather than practical needs. Since the revolution, the political system and its attributes, along with the persistence of a rentier economy, have seriously impeded the development of an effective progressive tax system.[20] Taxes constitute only 7 per cent of Iran's GDP, with 50 per cent of the population exempt from taxation and the remainder often engaging in tax evasion.[21] All *bonyads* and military-linked companies and businesses that control large parts of the economy have been granted tax-free status. In the face of ongoing fiscal inefficiency and declining oil revenue, Rouhani decided in 2014 to raise taxes and cut government expenditure. In December the *Majles* adopted a law to tax the aforementioned *bonyads* and military-linked companies. Even so, the revenue raised under the new law will amount to about 10 billion rials, or US$377 million (at the prevailing official rate of exchange) on an annual basis.[22] While part of the tax revenue was earmarked to be spent on building schools in disadvantaged areas, it will not necessarily make up for the government's falling income from oil.

Lastly, the Islamic Republic has had to contend with sociopolitical challenges to its economy. In addition, a 2006 International Monetary Fund (IMF) report states that Iran has the highest rate of brain drain of 90 countries measured, at an estimated cost to Iran of US$90 billion a year.[23] This trend evidently accelerated in subsequent years in the face of increased state authoritarianism, and social and economic difficulties. Adding to the list of the challenges with economic costs is the growth of drug addiction in the country. Despite the government's stringent measures to control the trafficking of drugs from neighbouring Afghanistan and Pakistan, the number of opium addicts has continued to rise. There is no precise figure available, but according to a report in *The Economist* (quoting Iranian official sources), two million people were addicted in 2013, although unofficial estimates put it at closer to five million.[24] Many Iranians believe that it has reached epidemic proportions in light of increased unemployment among youth, causing a massive social problem and at much opportunity and direct economic cost.

Relations with the United States and its European allies

US–Iranian hostilities and mutual distrust, as well as the fluctuating state of Iranian–European relations, which have experienced more ebbs than flows for more than 36 years, have taken a heavy toll on Iran. Apart from Cuba, no other country has been subjected to US sanctions for so long. The Iranian government and many of the country's citizens have partly adjusted to the regime of sanctions by developing a 'resistance economy'. The US sanctions, in combination with those imposed by the European Union, especially since 2012, have seriously affected Iran's international engagements and its economic and social development, while bringing increasing hardship for a majority of the country's population. In addition, these policies have helped to legitimate the conservative agenda and thereby to strengthen the *jihadis*' hold on economic and political power in a shrinking and increasingly isolated economy.

Apart from the ideological and political differences – or perhaps as a result of these – Iran's nuclear programme emerged as the key variable standing in the way of better relations with the West, the US in particular. The factors of mutual need and vulnerability finally led Presidents Barack Obama and Rouhani to act urgently in addressing the nuclear issue and thus to open the way for some kind of US–Iranian rapprochement. While resolution of the nuclear issue has been critical to normalizing Iran's political status and reintegrating it into the world political system, this objective may not be expected to entail a smooth transition into a US–Iranian rapprochement in the near future.

The interim nuclear deal reached between Iran and the Group of 5+1 in November 2013, which was to lead to a comprehensive agreement by 20 July 2014, signalled a serious willingness on the part of both Obama and Rouhani to transition their countries from the politics of hostility to a relationship of dialogue, understanding and negotiation. However, the depth of distrust and differences between Washington and Tehran prevented the parties from reaching a final agreement by the deadline. The two sides therefore found it useful to extend the deadline to 24 November 2014. As the deadline of the second extension approached, it became clear that the parties needed yet more time to close the gap on some substantive issues. Despite frantic negotiations in Oman between Zarif and US Secretary of State John Kerry in the week leading up to the expiration of the deadline, the two sides remained in disagreement over a number of issues. Nevertheless, having made such inroads, neither side found it expedient at that stage to walk out of the negotiations empty-handed. Despite the obstacles that remained to be overcome, both sides appeared eager to build on the progress that had been made, and thereby to avoid raising the alternative possibility of a military confrontation.

Consequently, they agreed once again to extend the deadline for 'political agreement' to 31 March 2015 and a final deal by the end of June 2015. Meanwhile, Iran was allowed to keep its nuclear facilities and uranium enrichment processes intact, and to continue to access US$700 million monthly in frozen assets during the extended period. While voicing optimism about the chances of a final agreement, Zarif and Kerry acknowledged the need for more time to iron out some of the remaining differences – a proposition that was immediately endorsed by both Rouhani and Khamenei. As for Israel, which has staunchly opposed the prospect of any nuclear agreement with Iran, it too breathed a sigh of relief. Prime Minister Benjamin Netanyahu proclaimed that no deal was better than a 'bad deal', and applauded the extension on the expectation that further negotiations would likewise prove unattainable.

Opposition from within the United States – particularly following the Republicans' landslide victory in the midterm gubernatorial elections in November 2014 – further complicated the delicate task of negotiations. Against the indications of American intelligence assessments, critics argued that the extension could only provide Tehran time to sneakily complete a nuclear bomb to the surprise of the West. Republicans in Congress accused Obama of letting Iran off the hook and called for fresh sanctions, which the Obama administration sought to stave off in pursuit of further diplomatic efforts. Although a veil of secrecy at the time surrounded the negotiations that led to the second extension, five issues emerged as clear sticking points.

The first was the level to which Iran was to be allowed to enrich uranium. The US and its allies ideally wanted Iran to limit enrichment to a level of 3 per cent – a level appropriate for civilian purposes, but well below that necessary for the development of nuclear bombs. This would be a level that Obama could sell to his domestic and regional critics. However, Iran had already achieved an enrichment level of 20 per cent, and the Iranian Supreme Leader, along with his hardline supporters, insisted that Iran should continue with its enrichment as an inalienable right. Rouhani could compromise on the issue only to the extent that he could secure a deal that he could sell domestically as well.

The second issue concerned the lifting of sanctions against Iran. Tehran wanted an immediate end to all sanctions, whereas the United States and its three European allies desired an incremental approach. The latter insisted that sanctions be lifted in proportion to Iran's fulfilment of the terms of the comprehensive agreement that the two sides may conclude.

The third issue related to stringent verification and certification measures, and specifically to the invasive inspections by the International Atomic Energy Agency (IAEA) of all Iranian nuclear facilities, including

127

Parchin, which the US and its three European allies as well as the IAEA suspected to be the site for possible nuclear testing for military purposes. Tehran viewed this demand as an impingement on its sovereignty and as unnecessary access to its sensitive military sites. It argued that it had already provided for sufficient and regular IAEA inspections of its nuclear facilities, and there was nothing more relevant at its sites for the agency or any other inspection team to investigate.

The fourth issue was linked to Tehran's concerns about Iran's overall national security and relations with the West, especially the United States. The Iranian leaders – from Khamenei to Rouhani – feel an acute sense of vulnerability in face of the fact that Iran is surrounded by nuclear powers, with Israel to the west, Pakistan to the east, Russia to the north as well as the US in the Gulf. The Islamic government has all along considered its security and that of Iran to be contingent upon its ability to effectively counter any internal challenge and external aggression. While Tehran believes that it has sufficient conventional military strength to deter any foreign attack, especially by Israel, it has been very conscious that it should only sign a final nuclear deal that could conform with its national security requirements. As part of this, Tehran has been keen to secure a commitment from the US that it would abandon its traditional policy goal of regime change and threat of military action towards Iran, and that it would ask Israel to do the same. It has also wanted the US to respect the legitimacy of the Islamic government and Iran's interests in the region and beyond, based on the principles of equality and mutual respect. Iran had also all along called for a region-wide regime of arms control that would include Israel as part of a nuclear-free zone in the Middle

East. While the nuclear disarmament of Israel is not something that the US and its partners in the Group of 5+1 would have put on the table, it was a card that Tehran could always play to call out diplomatic double standards, especially if it was pressured to make unacceptable concessions.

The fifth issue concerned Iran's quest for the return of all Iranian assets frozen in the United States since the advent of the Iranian Islamic government and the hostage crisis. This is an issue that Washington appeared reluctant to concede urgently.

The resolution of these issues was by no means easily achievable, but nor was it insurmountable. Provided that the two sides were genuinely interested in reaching a common position, based on mutual understanding and trust, it was possible. As such, the two sides finally reached what became known as the Lausanne framework agreement on 2 April 2015 for a final comprehensive nuclear deal to be finalized within three months. This was followed by intense political and technical negotiations between Iran and the Group of 5+1, involving many private and one-to-one discussions and dealings between Zarif and Kerry. While both sides were posturing to reach a mutually acceptable and saleable deal, they finally signed a comprehensive nuclear agreement or what was officially called 'The Joint Comprehensive Plan of Action' on 14 July 2015. The agreement essentially provided for curbing Tehran's possible ambitions to produce nuclear weapons in return for some important gains for Iran.

The key elements of the agreement committed Iran to reduce the stockpile of its low-enriched uranium by 98 percent to 300 kg for 15 years, to cut its centrifuges from 19,000 to 5,060, to allow vigorous inspection by the IAEA of its major nuclear sites for 25 years and in some cases permanently, and to accept continuation of UN sanctions on purchases of conventional weapons for five years and ballistic missiles for eight years. It also contained a 'snap back' clause for the re-imposition of sanctions within 60 days if an international panel finds Iran to be in breach of the agreement.

In return, under the agreement, the US-led Western, and UN economic and financial sanctions on Iran were to be lifted gradually (unfreezing some $100 billion of Iran's assets abroad), although after verification by the IAEA to ensure that Iran kept its end of the bargain. Iran was also to retain its right to enrich uranium, albeit at a level required for peaceful purposes – something that Tehran had always insisted to be the case – and to basically maintain its nuclear programme. This, together with Iran having achieved a desirable level of nuclear know-how, technological sophistication and infrastructural development, with no compelling reasons to cross the threshold to weaponize, meant that Tehran was well positioned to sign the agreement. The deal was based on substantial compromises, meeting the bottom lines of each side. With ratification and implementation of the agreement in good faith, it constitutes a win-win for both sides. It carries the potential to pave the way for a US-Iranian rapprochement at least in the medium to long run. Such a development would mark another milestone in US-Iranian relations with some significant regional implications, especially against the backdrop of the fact that the American and Iranian delegations have reportedly discussed a number of regional conflicts – ranging from those of Iraq and Syria to that of Yemen – on the sidelines of the nuclear negotiations and the possible cooperative role that they could play in addressing them. However, for this to materialize, there will be a need for more confidence-building measures at not only the bilateral, but also the regional level.

Regional situation

Iran's political fortunes, as we saw in chapter 4, have been closely tied to the changing dynamics within the regional landscape. Iran's future directions will also be determined by developments within the region. The Iranian Islamic government has serious concerns about Israel as a dominant military power with a brazen and defiant policy of threatening both Iran and its regional allies with military action. The Israeli leadership has too often shown a trigger-happy approach towards not only the Palestinians, but also Israel's neighbours, including the Iranian-backed Bashar al-Assad government in Syria and Hezbollah in Lebanon. Tehran has sought to counter Israel's anti-Iranian activities – including support for Kurdish independence in Iraq irrespective of the implications for the Kurdish population of Iran – by sustaining its organic links with the Syrian government and Hezbollah at all costs. Iran's ongoing support for these two regional enemies of America and Israel has considerably hampered possibilities for publicly declared military cooperation with the United States, particularly against the so-called Islamic State (IS).

Israel's hostility is complemented by the sectarian and geopolitical apprehension and distrust that Saudi Arabia and some of its Gulf Arab allies have harboured towards Iran. These states have particularly been concerned about Iran's Shi'a ideological disposition and a perceived threat from the country's military build-up and nuclear programme. To shore

Iran at the Crossroads

up their position against such a threat, apart from building their own defence forces, they have lately decided to do what they did to counter the Shah's military build-up in the mid-1970s: namely, to exercise their dominance in the Organization of the Petroleum Exporting Countries (OPEC) to limit Iran's income from its oil and thus restrain its military spending.[25] This was clearly evidenced in the position that Saudi Arabia as the leading OPEC producer and its smaller Gulf allies adopted in the late November 2014 OPEC meeting. While being capable of absorbing a reduction in their own oil revenue, they opposed Tehran's earnest call for a cut in oil production to boost the plummeting oil prices.[26] Meanwhile, the deepening Saudi–Pakistani strategic ties have become a growing source of concern for Tehran, which has reason to view both Saudi Arabia and Pakistan as its two main Sunni-dominated geopolitical competitors in the region. In addition, Iranian–Pakistani relations have been marred by growing cross-border problems, as discussed previously. All this has a significant bearing on Iranian strategic thinking.

Tehran's desire to position itself in such a way as to influence its immediate environment in pursuit of its strategic interests has been impeded by a regional situation that has become increasingly fraught with uncertainties. The rise of IS over swathes of Iraqi and Syrian territory with the goal of uniting the whole of the Muslim world, along with the US-led military response to this development, has confronted Iran with new strategic quandaries. While regarding IS as a serious threat to its interests in Iraq and Syria, Iran remains highly sceptical of the US-led and Gulf Cooperation Council-backed reintervention in Iraq and the unprecedented foray into Syria.

Iran's approach to combating IS has been two-pronged. On the one hand, as announced by Khamenei on 21 October 2014, it has insisted that Iraq can battle IS without foreign help.[27] On the other, it has been conscious of the growing convergence of its interests with those of the United States in opposition to IS and in support of the preservation of Iraq's sovereignty and territorial integrity. In this context, while Tehran has quietly cooperated with the US against IS in Iraq, it has also conducted its own anti-IS military operations in the country. Yet, Tehran has not found it expedient to formally coordinate its actions with those of the United States – a view replicated in Washington. The Deputy Chief of Staff of Iran's Armed Forces, Brigadier-General Massoud Jazayeri, made it clear on 3 December 2014 that there was to be no collaboration with the US. He said Iran considered the US responsible for Iraq's 'unrest and problems', adding that the US would 'definitely not have a place in the future of that country'.[28] Meanwhile, from Tehran's perspective, one consideration may be to contain and degrade IS rather than to eliminate it entirely for as long as it can extract political and strategic clout from portrayal of the group's Sunni extremism as an extension of Saudi-type Salafism. The rise of IS – facilitated in large part by Saudi financiers – provides Iran with a prime opportunity to discredit its major Sunni regional rival, and simultaneously to bolster Iran's international reputation as a relatively moderate bulwark against violent extremism. On the other hand, Iranian policymakers are painfully aware of the uncontrollable backlash that opening a Pandora's box of even more vehement sectarianism in the region could precipitate, and are wary of how it would affect both regional stability and Iran's own interests in the short and long term.

On the whole, the Iranian Supreme Leader and president appear to be united in the view that Iran's geopolitical interests are best served by restoration of the pre-IS regional status quo as a prelude to reconsolidation of Iraq and Syria as viable allies of Iran. In other words, their efforts are clearly directed towards maintaining Iran's pre-IS regional influence, and thus preserving and strengthening the Tehran–Baghdad–Damascus–Hezbollah axis as critical to Iran's national security within the Middle East security complex. However, to score well on this front, Iran needs improved relations with the United States just as much as the United States requires good relations with Iran to be able to regain some of its past geopolitical influence as a credible and influential actor in the Middle East.

As the situation stands, rectification of the Islamic system of governance, the dire economic situation and improvement of relations with the United States and its major European allies, as well as the changing regional and international situation, are major challenges with which Rouhani will have to deal. The success of one requires positive accomplishment and reinforcement in the others. As such, these issues are collectively set to influence Iran's domestic and foreign policy direction in the coming years.

6

Conclusion

Since its creation in 1979, the Islamic Republic of Iran has remained locked in a cycle whereby its movements have been propelled by both domestic gridlock and international hostility. Iran's view of itself is shaped not only by historical pride and resilience, but also by its experiences as a state whose existence in modern times, especially since the rise of its Islamic government, has been constantly under threat. In other words, the worldview of the country's ruling clerical stratum is not just guided by Ayatollah Ruhollah Khomeini's Shi'a Islamic vision. It is also shaped, in no small part, by eight years of war with Iraq, the US and Israeli threat of regime change and military action, US-led Western sanctions, and regional Arab apprehension. All this has fed into and legitimized the isolationist and uncompromising stance of the dominant conservative factions within Iran's governing power structure. The behaviour of these factions, in turn, has served to further engrain the image of Iran amongst the US conservative forces as an irrational and dangerous state and to justify their own hardline policy behaviour towards the country, a policy in which Israel has taken much comfort.

However, the democratic and pluralistic dimension

135

of the Iranian Islamic political system and the social, political and economic failings of the *jihadi* factions and foreign policy complications have periodically enabled the rise of pragmatic and reform-minded leaders. Hassan Rouhani, Mohammad Khatami and, to a lesser extent, Hashemi Rafsanjani have each sought to improve Iran's relations with the outside world as part of a broader attempt to instigate reforms within Iran. Each of these presidents approached the United States with the goal of achieving a degree of reconciliation. In doing so, they often placed their personal political legitimacy on the line. By refusing to respond to Khatami's and Rafsanjani's overtures, Washington gave credence to the *jihadis*' depictions of the United States as an imperialist, hegemonic power interested only in dominance and exploitation, not in negotiation and reconciliation. The US's post-Second World War interventions in support of the Shah's regime and its refusal to recognize Khomeini's Islamic government as legitimate, which remains entrenched within the Iranian national memory, provide a means by which *jihadis* can continue to substantiate their negative view of the United States and its regional allies, Israel in particular.

Iran today stands at a critical crossroads. On the one hand, the country's Islamic government has moved on from its early radical revolutionary years. While maintaining a strong adherence to Shi'a Islam as defined by Khomeini, this has become largely a source of policy justification rather than a policy guide. In the meantime, Iran has grown reasonably self-assured, confident and pragmatic. It is no longer as fearful of domestic or external threats that it cannot handle. Although continuing to operate within Khomeini's *jihadi* and *ijtihadi* framework, it has increasingly found it realistic to lean towards the latter. On the other hand, incongruity within its system of governance, economic and social stagnation, and US-led Western sanctions and international isolation, as well as a regional Arab perception of Iran as threatening, have confronted it with serious domestic difficulties and foreign policy roadblocks, impeding opportunities for thoroughgoing but much-needed reform.

Meanwhile, the United States and Israel are no longer in as strong a position in the Middle East as they were before the turn of the twenty-first century. The Afghanistan and Iraq Wars, coupled with the inability to be a determining player in the Syrian conflict, to secure a resolution of the Israeli–Palestinian conflict, or to contain, let alone eliminate, the extremist forces acting in the name of Islam – from al-Qaeda to IS – as well as the failure to remain consistent in support of democratic forces in the wake of the 'Arab Spring', have substantially reduced America's past geopolitical dominance in the region. Israel is in a similar predicament. Its growing domestic political and economic woes, its international isolation, largely due to its refusal to reach a final settlement with the Palestinians on the basis of a two-state solution, and its increasingly contemptuous relations with its main backer, the United States,[1] have markedly diminished its credibility as a respectable and constructive player on the regional and global stage. These developments, combined with the overlapping US–Iranian security interests in the face of such extremist groups as IS and al-Qaeda, as well as the July 2015 nuclear agreement to end sanctions and undertake serious political, economic and social reforms, have provided Iran's ruling clerics with both opportunities and challenges in their choice of paths in the short and long term.

One path is where the *jihadi* cluster is allowed to

maintain its dominance over Iranian domestic politics and seeks to press on with hardline foreign policy priorities and objectives. This scenario is likely to increase instability by deepening regional sectarian tensions and rivalries, and cementing divisions within Iran's own political elite. Such a course cannot only potentially exacerbate the power struggle between the *jihadi/ ijtihadi* clusters, but can also lend itself to infighting among the various *jihadi* factions themselves. This, in turn, has the potential to destabilize the entire Islamic political system and demolish its legitimacy.

Another option is if the Iranian polity moves down the path of *ijtihadi* Islamic politics and transformative changes in pursuit of more pluralistic and open politics, socioeconomic reform within Iran and reconciliation with the outside world, especially the United States. Domestic reformation is likely to generate the necessary conditions and opportunities not only for deeper state–society relationships, but also for mitigating the potential security challenges posed by the numerous minority ethnic and religious groups in the country, such as the Sunni Baluchis, Kurds, Arabs and members of the Baha'i faith. If it continues to move in this direction, the Iranian regime has the potential to address such deep-seated issues as system incongruity, corruption, patronage, an undiversified economy and foreign policy obstacles. This is what Rouhani seems to be most interested in achieving, provided that he can overcome the challenges that arise from these very issues. Rouhani certainly has his work cut out for him.

Whatever reforms Rouhani wants to accomplish, they cannot be effected without addressing Iran's security concerns; in particular, they cannot take place in the context of a hostile international climate. This is where the role of the United States and its major

Western allies comes to the fore. Reform in the Islamic Republic is not simply a question of what Tehran can do to loosen its fist. It is also an issue of how far the US government and its main European counterparts can move forward to reconcile their interests with those of the Iranian Islamic government and find common ground. While European leaders may have more room for flexibility in this respect, the same cannot be said about President Barack Obama. To make the necessary compromises, the president has to navigate his way around the Israeli lobby, the forces of the American right and the Republican-dominated Congress. Only recently, the Congress passed the US–Israel Strategic Partnership Act of 2014, which the president signed into law, and this was in no small measure due to the efforts of the Israeli lobby on Capitol Hill.

Despite the difficulties for Presidents Rouhani and Obama, both sides currently have a more reasonable window of opportunity to move their countries towards a US–Iranian rapprochement than at any time since the advent of the Iranian Islamic government. The Rouhani government buzzes with optimism and Foreign Minister Mohammad Javad Zarif has repeatedly indicated a strong preference for improved relations with the United States, despite domestic and regional opposition.

If the opportunity that has arisen in the wake of the signing of the nuclear agreement is not utilized effectively, both sides have much to lose. Rouhani would not be able to press on with his reform agenda, and to end fruitfully the burden of Iran's estrangement from the West, especially the US. The issue has gained greater potency when considered in the light of the substantial decrease in oil prices and Iran's declining income from this source. Saudi blocking of the Iranian request for a reduction in oil production in order to raise oil prices in the December 2014 meeting of the Organization of Petroleum Exporting Countries (OPEC) has caused much angst in Iran. At the same time, this Saudi approach may urge Tehran to do whatever possible, as quickly as possible, to treat the signed nuclear deal as a prelude to possible restoration of relations with Washington.

Similarly, in the event that the current efforts fail to produce substantial results, President Obama would be unable to achieve his objective to reset US–Iranian relations for the sake of regional stability and America's interests in the Middle East. Obama's path to normalizing relations may prove to be even more complicated than that facing Rouhani. In addition to overcoming domestic opposition, Obama must provide reassurance not only to Israel, but also to a number of other regional allies, including Turkey, Saudi Arabia and Egypt, where every American move for better relations with Iran could easily cut across conflicting perceived interests. For example, while the United States' interests have come to overlap those of Iran in opposing IS, Iran and Turkey are at loggerheads in Syria, with Tehran supporting and Ankara opposing the Bashar al-Assad regime. At the same time as America is standing by Ankara and Saudi Arabia and its Arab allies, these actors may well only want IS to be contained rather than eliminated, because of its anti-Tehran and anti-Damascus stance.

A US–Iranian rapprochement, or lack of it, possesses the potential to profoundly affect Iranian domestic and foreign policy settings and the Middle Eastern geostrategic landscape. It is therefore no wonder that the Obama and Rouhani leaderships are keen to see their efforts culminate in fruitful outcomes based on compromises that enable the two sides to claim mutual benefit and are marketable to their domestic opponents. Iran and the United States are now at the crossroads of either moving forward to reset their relations or missing an unprecedented opportunity to achieve this objective.

The configuration of issues and forces, especially in the wake of the signed nuclear agreement, favours the possibility of re-setting relations, provided that the two sides are able to wear the necessary domestic risks and to take the bold steps required to show their opponents that a major breakthrough in Iranian–US relations will bring tangible benefits. This is not to underestimate the difficulties that lie ahead. It is merely to suggest that a rapprochement between the two sides cannot be discounted in the medium term. Both sides have much to gain from such a development and could be expected to do whatever possible to move in this direction during the remaining presidency of Obama – a Republican administration in the US may prove to be less conciliatory.

The United States and Iran have travelled a considerable way from the days of mutual demonization and incrimination. By the force of parallel vulnerabilities and leverage, they cannot now easily afford to turn the clock back and abandon what they have achieved so far. The more they succeed in moving forward with tangible benefits for both sides, the more they may also be in a position either to persuade many of their domestic and regional critics to appreciate the fruits of their efforts or to let them fall in with the caravan of their achievements.

If the United States and the Socialist Republic of Vietnam could reconcile after America's Vietnam fiasco, and if the US is able to restore relations following some six decades of enmity with Cuba, a similar development with Iran is not to be viewed as insurmountable. After all, the American and Iranian experiences have not been as damaging as those that had underpinned US relations with Vietnam and Cuba.

The Middle East has entered one of the most volatile and bloody periods in its modern historical evolution. Any normalization of US–Iranian relations can only have a stabilizing effect and help the resolution of numerous problematic issues that have dogged the region for so long. Without Iranian involvement and use of Iranian leverage, none of the major regional problems can be satisfactorily addressed. All indications suggest that the Iranian Islamic government has achieved long-term durability. The best option available now is not only for a US–Iranian rapprochement to materialize, but also for all regional forces to accept it as a reality and to focus on it as a critical building block for regional cooperation and stability. The alternative is a continuation of volatility and unpredictability, which has made the Middle East a chronic source of tension, anxiety and conflict in world politics. The US and its allies are seriously concerned about the rise of China as a world power and may see America's pivot to the Asia-Pacific region as a long-term necessity. However, the Middle East's vulnerability to extremism and violent instability carries the potential to drag the focus away from Asia and from the work that needs to be done to consolidate a new viable world order.

Notes

Chapter 1 Introduction

1 Jimmy Carter, Tehran, Iran Toasts of the President and the Shah at a State Dinner. 31 December 1977; available at: *The American Presidency Project*, www. presidency.ucsb.edu/ws/?pid=7080.

Chapter 2 From Empire to Islamic Republic

1 Abul-Qasim Ferdowsi (AD 940–1020).

2 Nezami Ganjavi (AD 1140–1202).

3 See Pierre Briant, *From Cyrus to Alexander: A History of the Persian Empire* (Winona Lake, IN: Eisenbrauns, 2002).

4 A recent analysis of the decline of the Sassanids and the continuity of Iranian identity after the Arab-Islamic conquests can be found in Parvaneh Pourshariati, *Decline and Fall of the Sasanian Empire: The Sasanian-Parthian Confederacy and the Arab Conquest of Iran* (London: I. B. Tauris, 2008).

5 Roger Savory, *Iran Under the Safavids* (Cambridge: Cambridge University Press, 1980).

6   See Rudi Matthee, *Persia in Crisis: Safavid Decline and the Fall of Isfahan* (London: I. B. Tauris, 2012).

7   Firuz Kazemzadeh, *Russia and Britain in Persia: Imperial Ambitions in Qajar Iran* (New Haven, CT: Yale University Press, 2013).

8   Homa Katouzian, *The Persians: Ancient, Mediaeval and Modern Iran* (New Haven, CT: Yale University Press, 2009), pp. 3–18.

9   See, for example, Evaleila Pesaran, *Iran's Struggle for Economic Independence: Reform and Counter-Reform in the Post-Revolutionary Era* (New York: Routledge, 2011).

10 For a discussion of the political role of the *ulama* during the Qajar dynasty, see Hamid Algar, *Religion and State in Iran, 1785–1906: The Role of the Ulama in the Qajar Period* (Berkeley: University of California Press, 1969). An in-depth and multilayered account of the Constitutional revolution is available in Janet Afary, *The Iranian Constitutional Revolution, 1906–1911: Grassroots Democracy, Social Democracy, and the Origins of Feminism* (New York: Columbia University Press, 1996).

11 Amin Saikal, *The Rise and Fall of the Shah: Iran from Autocracy to Religious Rule* (Princeton: Princeton University Press, 2009), p. 16.

12 Ervand Abrahamian, *Iran Between Two Revolutions* (Princeton: Princeton University Press, 1982).

13 Amin Saikal, Kemalism: Its influences on Iran and Afghanistan. *International Journal of Turkish Studies* 2(2) 1982.

14 For a good discussion of Reza Shah's period, see Ali M. Ansari, *Modern Iran Since 1921: The Pahlavis and After* (London: Longman, 2003), ch. 2.

15 For details, see Bruce R. Kuniholm, *The Origins of the Cold War in the Near East: Great Power Conflict and*

Diplomacy in Iran, Turkey, and Greece (Princeton: Princeton University Press, 1980).

16 For a detailed account of Mossadeq's life and activities, see Mohammad Mossadeq, *Mossadeq's Memoirs*, trans. S. H. Amin and H. Katouzian (London: JEBHE, National Movement of Iran, 1988).

17 Saikal, *The Rise and Fall of the Shah*, pp. 35–45.

18 See Mary Ann Heiss, *Empire and Nationhood: The United States, Great Britain, and Iranian Oil, 1950–1954* (New York: Columbia University Press, 1997) for an in-depth account of the oil nationalization crisis and its relation to US and British foreign policy.

19 For a detailed discussion, see Stephen Kinzer, *All the Shah's Men: An American Coup and the Roots of Middle East Terror* (Hoboken, NJ: John Wiley & Sons, 2003).

20 For a critical view of the Shah's re-assumption of the Peacock Throne and America's role, see Bahman Nirumand, *Iran: The New Imperialism in Action*, trans. Leonard Mins (New York: Monthly Review Press, 1969).

21 See Mohammad Reza Pahlavi, *Mission for My Country* (New York: McGraw Hill, 1961), which devotes an entire chapter to the theme of positive nationalism. See also Ansari, *Modern Iran Since 1921*, chs 5–6.

22 On the Kennedy administration's relationship with the Shah, see James A. Bill, *The Eagle and the Lion: The Tragedy of American–Iranian Relations* (New Haven, CT: Yale University Press, 1988), ch. 4. For the Shah's perspective on the White Revolution, see Mohammad Reza Shah Pahlavi, *Answer to History* (Toronto: Irwin & Co., 1980), ch. 9.

23 Marvin Zonis, *The Political Elite of Iran* (Princeton: Princeton University Press, 1971), p. 13.

24 Mohammad Reza Pahlavi, *Towards the Great*

Civilization, in Persian (Tehran: Pahlavi Library Publication, 1977).

25 Abrahamian, *Iran Between Two Revolutions*, pp. 435–6.

26 For a comprehensive discussion of the Shah's accelerated modernization programme, see Saikal, *The Rise and Fall of the Shah*, Part 2.

27 For a detailed biography of Khomeini and an account of his rise and popularity, see Baqer Moin, *Khomeini: Life of the Ayatollah* (London: I. B. Tauris, 1999).

28 For Khomeini's early views, see Ervand Abrahamian, *Khomeinism: Essays on the Islamic Republic* (London: I. B. Tauris, 1993).

29 For a detailed analysis of the origins and evolution of the Iranian revolution, see Said Amir Arjomand, *The Turban for the Crown: The Islamic Revolution in Iran* (Oxford: Oxford University Press, 1988).

30 *Daytona Beach Morning Journal*, 8 December 1978.

Chapter 3   The Islamic Order

1 For a discussion of Khomeini's early views, see Ervand Abrahamian, *Khomeinism: Essays on the Islamic Republic* (London: I. B. Tauris, 1993).

2 *Le Monde*, 17 October 1978.

3 See Abbas Milani, *Eminent Persians: The Men and Women Who Made Modern Iran, 1941–1979*, vol. 1 (New York: Syracuse University Press, 2008), p. 348.

4 For details on the life and ideas of Khomeini, see Baqer Moin, *Khomeini: Life of the Ayatollah* (London: I. B. Tauris, 1999).

5 For details in English, see Ayatollah Ruhollah Khomeini, *Islamic Government* (Springfield, VA: National Technical Information Service, 1979).

6   Amin Saikal, *Zone of Crisis: Afghanistan, Pakistan, Iran and Iraq* (London: I. B. Tauris, 2014), pp. 107–13.
7   *Le Monde*, 9 January 1979.
8   A detailed analysis of the Constitution is provided in Asghar Schirazi, *The Constitution of Iran: Politics and the State in the Islamic Republic* (London: I. B. Tauris, 1998).
9   Vali Nasr, *The Shia Revival: How Conflicts within Islam Will Shape the Future* (New York: W. W. Norton & Co., 2006), pp. 130–1.
10 The terms *jihadi* and *ijtihadi* need to be understood strictly as they are defined in this book, rather than in any other sense.
11 For the reception of Khomeini's theory among the Iranian *ulama*, see Hamid Enayat, Iran: Khumayni's concept of the 'Guardianship of the Jurisconsult'. In: James P. Piscatori (ed.), *Islam in the Political Process* (New York: Cambridge University Press, 1983).
12 For Bani-Sadr's perspective on the revolution, circumstances of his departure for exile and his differences with Khomeini, see Abol-Hassan Bani Sadr, *My Turn to Speak: Iran, the Revolution and Secret Deals with the US* (New York: Brassey's, 1991).
13 See John L. Esposito (ed.), *The Oxford Encyclopedia of the Modern Islamic World*, vol. 1 (Oxford: Oxford University Press, 1995), sv. '*bunyad*', pp. 235–7.
14 Eva Rakel, Conglomerates in Iran: The political economy of Islamic foundations. In: Alex E. Fernández Jilberto and Barbara Hogenboom (eds), *Big Business and Economic Development: Conglomerates and Economic Groups in Developing Countries and Transition Economies under Globalisation* (New York: Routledge, 2007); Abbas William Samii, The Iranian nuclear issue and informal networks. *Naval War College Review* 59(1) 2006.

15 Amin Saikal, *The Rise and Fall of the Shah: Iran from Autocracy to Religious Rule* (Princeton: Princeton University Press, 2009), p. xxvi.

16 For a Western perspective on this particular issue, see Henry Kissinger, *World Order: Reflections on the Character of Nations and the Course of History* (New York: Allen Lane, 2014), ch. 4.

17 An Islamist is a person who believes in Islam as an ideology of political and social transformation of his/her society. There are those Islamists who sanction the use of violence as a means to achieve their objectives; some of them are better known as *jihadis* or 'radical Islamists', who constitute a small minority in the Muslim world. In contrast to this cluster are those who reject any form of violence as a means to achieving their goals; they are better known as *ijtihadis* or 'moderate Islamists', who form the bulk of Muslim thinkers and activists. See Amin Saikal, *Islam and the West: Conflict or Cooperation?* (London: Palgrave Macmillan, 2003), pp. 25–9.

18 For a discussion of reformism in Iran, see Shireen T. Hunter, Islamic reformist discourse in Iran. In: Shireen T. Hunter (ed.), *Reformist Voices of Islam: Mediating Islam and Modernity* (New York: Routledge, 2009).

19 For Khatami's views, see Mohammad Khatami, *Islam, Dialogue and Civil Society* (Canberra: Centre for Arab and Islamic Studies, Australian National University, 2000); and for a discussion of Soroush's early writings, see Ali Mirsepassi, *Democracy in Modern Iran: Islam, Culture, and Political Change* (New York: New York University Press, 2010), pp. 87–90.

20 See Ray Takeyh, *Hidden Iran: Paradox and Power in the Islamic Republic* (New York: Times Books, 2006), ch. 1.

21 Mehdi Moslem, *Factional Politics in Post-Khomeini Iran* (New York: Syracuse University Press, 2002), pp. 68–9.

22 See Amin Saikal, The politics of factionalism in Iran. Workshop paper in Jerrod D. Green, Frederic Wehrey and Charles Wolf Jr (eds), *Understanding Iran* (Santa Monica, CA: RAND, 2009). See also Maziar Behrooz, Factionalism in Iran under Khomeini. *Middle Eastern Studies* 27(4) 1991.

23 See International Crisis Group, *Iran: The Struggle for the Revolution's Soul*, Middle East Report No. 5, 5 August 2002, pp. 16–19.

24 See Said Amir Arjomand, *After Khomeini: Iran under His Successors* (Oxford: Oxford University Press, 2009), ch. 3; Anoushirvan Ehteshami, *After Khomeni: The Iranian Second Republic* (London: Taylor & Francis, 2002).

25 *Chicago Tribune*, 21 July 1988.

26 Adam Tarock, Iran–Western Europe relations on the mend. *British Journal of Middle Eastern Studies* 26(1) 1999, 59–60.

27 Ali M. Ansari, Iran under Ahmadinejad: The politics of confrontation, *Adelphi Papers* 47/393 (Abingdon: Routledge for the International Institute for Strategic Studies, 2007), p. 16.

28 For a detailed discussion of the policy of 'dual containment', see Kenneth M. Pollack, *The Persian Puzzle: The Conflict Between Iran and America* (New York: Random House, 2004), pp. 259–73; and for Israel's role in the Clinton administration's foreign policy towards Iran, see Trita Parsi, *Treacherous Alliance: The Secret Dealings of Israel, Iran, and the United States* (New Haven, CT: Yale University Press, 2007), chs 14 and 15.

29 See Zbigniew Brzezinski, Brent Scowcroft, and Richard Murphy, Differentiated containment. *Foreign Affairs* 76(3) 1997.

30 The most detailed and balanced analysis of Iran's nuclear programme is David Patrikarakos, *Nuclear Iran: The Birth of an Atomic State* (London: I. B. Tauris, 2012).

31 Dobbins's account of this episode may be found in James Dobbins, Negotiating with Iran: Reflections from personal experience. *Washington Quarterly* 33(1) 2010.

32 See Robert Gates, *Duty: Memoirs of a Secretary at War* (New York: Alfred A. Knopf, 2014), pp. 185–6.

33 See Bahram Rajaee, Deciphering Iran: The political evolution of the Islamic Republic and US foreign policy after September 11. *Comparative Studies of South Asia, Africa and the Middle East* 24(1) 2004.

34 For more details on the life, character and politics of Ahmadinejad, see Ansari, Iran under Ahmadinejad; Anoushirvan Ehteshami and Mahjoob Zweiri, *Iran and the Rise of Its Neoconservatives: The Politics of Tehran's Silent Revolution* (London: I. B. Tauris, 2007); Kasra Naji, *Ahmadinejad: The Secret History of Iran's Radical Leader* (Berkeley: University of California Press, 2008).

35 The circumstances of Ahmadinejad's victory are treated more extensively in Ehteshami and Zweiri, *Iran and the Rise of Its Neoconservatives*, ch. 3.

36 For an evaluation of Ahmadinejad's first presidency, see Michael Axworthy, *Iran: Empire of the Mind: A History from Zoroaster to the Present Day* (London: Penguin, 2008), ch. 9.

37 Maaike Warnaar, *Iranian Foreign Policy during Ahmadinejad: Ideology and Actions* (New York: Palgrave Macmillan, 2013), chs 4 and 5.

38 For a detailed discussion, see Naji, *Ahmadinejad*, esp. chs 4–6.

39 Amin Saikal, The roots of Iran's election crisis. *Survival: Global Politics and Strategy* 51(5) 2009, 97–8.

40 *Iran News*, 29 October 2013.
41 Arron Merat, Rouhani deals with Ahmadinejad's economic legacy. *Al Monitor*, 11 September 2013, available at: www.al-monitor.com/pulse/fr/originals/2013/09/ ahmadinejad-leaves-rouhani-economic-problems.html.
42 Ramin Jahanbegloo, The two sovereignties and the legitimacy crisis in Iran. *Constellations* 17(1) 2010, 28.
43 Thomas Erdbrink, Iranian leader rebuffs Ahmadinejad over official's dismissal. *Washington Post*, 20 April 2011.
44 Julian Borger, Khamenei's son takes control of Iran's anti-protest militia. *Guardian*, 8 July 2009; Jeffrey Fleishman, Iran Supreme Leader's son seen as power broker with big ambitions. *Los Angeles Times*, 25 June 2009.

Chapter 4   Rouhani's Presidency and US–Iranian Relations

1 For further information on Iran during the Cold War, see Amin Saikal, Islamism, the Iranian revolution, and the Soviet invasion of Afghanistan. In: Melvyn P. Leffler and Odd Arne Westad (eds), *The Cambridge History of the Cold War*, vol. 3: *Endings* (Cambridge: Cambridge University Press, 2009), pp. 112–20.
2 See Dominic Sandbrook, After the revolution. *New Statesman*, 16 June 2009; David Farber, *Taken Hostage: The Iran Hostage Crisis and America's First Encounter with Radical Islam* (Princeton: Princeton University Press, 2005), ch. 3.
3 See Kenneth M. Pollack, *The Persian Puzzle: The Conflict Between Iran and America* (New York: Random House, 2004), p. 146.
4 See, for example, Farber, *Taken Hostage*; David Patrick Houghton, *US Foreign Policy and the Iran Hostage*

Crisis (Cambridge: Cambridge University Press, 2001); Gary Sick, *All Fall Down: America's Tragic Encounter with Iran* (New York: Random House, 1985); James A. Bill, *The Eagle and the Lion: The Tragedy of American-Iranian Relations* (New Haven, CT: Yale University Press, 1988).

5 For a detailed discussion, see Amin Saikal, The United States and Persian Gulf security. *World Policy Journal* 9(3) 1992.

6 For a discussion on the Iran–Iraq war, see Dilip Hiro, *The Longest War: The Iran–Iraq Military Conflict* (London: Grafton, 1989); Efraim Karsh, *The Iran–Iraq War: 1980–1988* (Oxford: Osprey Publishing, 2002); Stephen C. Pelletiere, *The Iran–Iraq War: Chaos in a Vacuum* (New York: Praeger, 1992).

7 See Alan Friedman, *Spider's Web: The Secret History of How the White House Illegally Armed Iraq* (New York: Bantam Books, 1993).

8 James G. Blight et al., *Becoming Enemies: US–Iran Relations and the Iran–Iraq War, 1979–1988* (Lanham, MD: Rowman & Littlefield, 2012).

9 R. K. Ramazani, Iran's foreign policy: Contending orientations. *Middle East Journal* 43(2) 1989; Shireen T. Hunter, Iran and the spread of revolutionary Islam. *Third World Quarterly* 10(2) 1988.

10 See Augustus Richard Norton, *Hezbollah: A Short History* (Princeton: Princeton University Press, 2007).

11 Hunter, Iran and the spread of revolitionary Islam.

12 Jane Hunter, Israeli arms sales to Iran. *Washington Report on Middle East Affairs*, November 1986, p. 2.

13 For a detailed treatment of the Iran-Contra Affair, see Ann Wroe, *Lives, Lies and the Iran-Contra Affair* (London: I. B. Tauris, 1992).

14 For a discussion of the US approach to, and relationship with, Iraq before and after Saddam Hussein's rule,

see Amin Saikal, *Zone of Crisis: Afghanistan, Pakistan, Iran and Iraq* (London: I. B. Tauris, 2014), ch. 5.

15 Trita Parsi, *Treacherous Alliance: The Secret Dealings of Israel, Iran, and the United States* (New Haven, CT: Yale University Press, 2007), pp. 130–48.

16 Elaine Sciolino, Iran offers trade on hostages, but US is cautious. *New York Times*, 24 October 1989.

17 For more details, see Parsi, *Treacherous Alliance*.

18 For a detailed discussion, see F. Gregory Gause III, The illogic of dual containment. *Foreign Affairs* 73(2) 1994.

19 For a detailed discussion, see Saikal, The United States and Persian Gulf security.

20 Zbigniew Brzezinski, Brent Scowcroft and Richard Murphy, Differentiated containment. *Foreign Affairs* 76(3) 1997.

21 Mohammad Khatami, *Dialogue and the New Millennium*, Address Delivered to the Thirtieth General Conference of the United Nations Educational Scientific and Cultural Organization (UNESCO), Paris, 29 October 1999, p. 2.

22 Mohammad Khatami, *Islam, Dialogue and Civil Society* (Canberra: Centre for Arab and Islamic Studies, Australian National University, 2000), p. 2.

23 For the amount of Iranian aid pledged and reimbursed between 2002 and 2010, see Amin Saikal, Afghanistan's geographic possibilities. *Survival: Global Politics and Strategy* 56(3) 2014, 150.

24 Bush's 'evil axis' comment stirs critics. *BBC News*, 2 February 2002.

25 National Commission on Terrorist Attacks Upon the United States, The 9/11 Commission Report. 22 July 2004, p. 241, available at: www.9-11commission.gov/report/.

26 Shireen T. Hunter, *Iran's Foreign Policy in the Post-Soviet Era: Resisting the New International Order* (Santa

Barbara, CA: Praeger, 2010), pp. 63–8, 96–9. For a detailed discussion of Ahmadinejad's presidency, see Ali M. Ansari, Iran under Ahmadinejad: The politics of confrontation. *Adelphi Papers* 47/393 (Abingdon: Routledge for the International Institute for Strategic Studies, 2007).

27 For a recent analysis of Iran's nuclear programme, see David Patrikarakos, *Nuclear Iran: The Birth of an Atomic State* (London: I. B. Tauris, 2012).

28 Gawdat Bahgat, Nuclear proliferation: The Islamic Republic of Iran. *Iranian Studies* 39(3) 2006.

29 For details of Rouhani's views, see Hassan Rouhani, *Rawaiti-e Tadbir wa Omid* [Narration of Foresight and Hope] (Tehran: Center for Strategic Research, 2013).

30 Andrew Torchia, Politics, markets complicate Rouhani's rescue of Iran economy. *Reuters*, 1 May 2014.

31 Jason Rezalan, Iran's Supreme Leader, Ayatollah Ali Khamenei, endorses diplomacy over militarism. *Washington Post*, 17 September 2013.

32 Office of the Press Secretary, Videotape remarks by the President in celebration of Nowruz. 20 March 2009, available at: www.whitehouse.gov/the_press_office/ VIDEOTAPED-REMARKS-BY-THE-PRESIDENT-IN-CELEBRATION-OF-NOWRUZ

33 See John Limbert, The Obama administration. In: Robin Wright (ed.), *The Iran Primer: Power, Politics, and US Policy* (Washington, DC: United States Institute of Peace, 2010), p. 146.

34 *Guardian*, 25 October 2010.

35 For details, see Amin Saikal, Iraq: Elite fragmentation, Islam and democracy. In: Shahram Akbarzadeh, et al. (eds), *American Democracy Promotion in the Changing Middle East: From Bush to Obama* (London: Routledge, 2013).

36 Mark N. Katz, Why Russia won't play ball on Iran. *The Diplomat*, 23 June 2012.

37 George G. Eberling, *Future Oil Demands of China, India, and Japan: Policy Scenarios and Implications* (Lanham, MD: Lexington Books, 2014), p. 61.

38 India oil imports from Iran jump sharply in 2014. *Economic Times*, 16 January 2015.

39 Amin Saikal, The promises of a US-Iranian rapprochement. *ABC News Australia*, 25 November 2013.

40 For a detailed discussion, see Robert Einhorn, A justified extension for Iran nuclear talks, but hard choices ahead. Brookings, 19 July 2014, available at: www.brookings.edu/blogs/iran-at-saban/posts/2014/07/19-iran-nuclear-talks-extended-hard-choices-enrichment.

41 For an example of opposition within the *Majles* and grilling of Foreign Minister Nazif, see the report in *Gulf in the Media*, 7 January 2015.

42 William Booth, Israel's Netanyahu calls Iran deal 'historic mistake'. *Washington Post*, 24 November 2013.

43 'Cut off head of snake', Saudis told US on Iran. *Reuters*, 29 November 2010.

44 Jason Burke, Riyadh will build nuclear weapons if Iran gets them, Saudi prince warns. *Guardian*, 29 June 2011.

Chapter 5   The Complex Road Ahead

1 Iran's Rouhani calls Israel 'old wound' on Islamic world. *BBC News*, 2 August 2013.

2 *BBC News* (Persian edition), 26 July 2014, available at: www.bbc.co.uk/persian/iran/2014/07/140726_ran_rouhani_friday_prayer_qods_day.

3 Scott Lucas, Blow to Rouhani as parliament dismisses science minister. *EA World View*, 21 August 2014.

4 Jahangir Amuzegar, *Iran's Economy under the Islamic Republic* (London: I. B. Tauris, 1993), p. 17.

5   Eva Patricia Rakel, The political elite in the Islamic Republic of Iran: From Khomeini to Ahmadinejad. *Comparative Studies of South Asia, Africa and the Middle East* 29(1) 2009.

6   See Suzanne Maloney, Agents or obstacles? Parastatal foundations and challenges for Iranian development. In: Parvin Alizadeh (ed.), *The Economy of Iran: The Dilemmas of an Islamic State* (London: I. B. Tauris, 2000); John L. Esposito (ed.), *The Oxford Encyclopedia of the Modern Islamic World*, vol. 1 (Oxford: Oxford University Press, 1995), sv. '*bunyad*', pp. 235–7.

7   For more on the wealth of the clerical elite, see Paul Klebnikov, Millionaire mullahs. *Forbes*, 21 July 2003 and Ali A. Saeidi, The accountability of para-governmental organizations (*bonyads*): The case of Iranian foundations. *Iranian Studies* 37(3) 2004.

8   Jahangir Amuzegar, Iran's economy in turmoil. *Carnergie Endowment for International Peace*, 18 March 2010.

9   World Bank, Iran overview, available at: www.worldbank.org/en/country/iran/overview.

10 Heidi Moore, Sanctions are pushing Iran towards nuclear talks, just not US sanctions. *Guardian*, 24 October 2012; Steve Hargreaves, Iraq oil production surpasses Iran. *CNN Money*, 10 August 2012.

11 Golnar Motevalli, Rouhani: Iran budget to face short-term pressure from oil. *The Daily Star*, 8 December 2014.

12 For a discussion of Iran's dependence on oil and its political ramifications, see Massoud Karshenas and Hassan Hakimian, Managing oil resources and economic diversification in Iran. In: Homa Katouzian and Hossein Shahidi (eds), *Iran in the 21st Century: Politics, Economics and Conflict* (Abingdon, Oxon: Routledge, 2008); Elliot Hen-Tov, Understanding

Iran's new authoritarianism. *Washington Quarterly* 30(1) 2006–7.

13 IISS (International Institute for Strategic Studies), *The Military Balance 2014* (London: Routledge, 2014), p. 3018.

14 Iran to hike military spending despite 'tight' budget. *World Bulletin*, 8 December 2014.

15 Foreign investors in Iran growing: Official. *Islamic Republic News Agency*, 5 November 2014, available at: www.irna.ir/en/News/2783563/.

16 Scott Lucas, Rouhani makes a play for support with public votes – but on which issues? *EA Worldview*, 6 January 2015.

17 David Michel, Iran's environment: Greater threat than foreign foes. United States Institute of Peace, 28 October 2013, available at: iranprimer.usip.org/blog/2013/oct/28/iran%E2%80%99s-environment-greater-threat-foreign-foes.

18 Javad Amid, The dilemma of cheap food and self-sufficiency: The case of wheat in Iran. *Food Policy* 32(4) 2007.

19 Transparency International, Corruption by country/territory: Iran, available at: www.transparency.org/country#IRN

20 See Hossein Askari, Iran's slide to the bottom. *Asia Times Online*, 15 September 2010, available at: www.atimes.com/atimes/Middle_East/LI15Ako1.html; and World Bank, Iran country brief. September 2010, available at: siteresources.worldbank.org/INTIRAN/Resources/Iran_Web_brief.pdf.

21 Amuzegar, Iran's economy in turmoil.

22 Iran plans to tax religious foundations, army-linked firms. *The Daily Star*, 4 December 2014.

23 Frances Harrison, Huge cost of Iranian brain drain. *BBC News*, 8 January 2007.

24 Drug addiction in Iran: The other religion. *The Economist*, 17 August 2013.
25 For details, see Amin Saikal, *The Rise and Fall of the Shah: Iran from Autocracy to Religious Rule* (Princeton: Princeton University Press, 2009), pp. 98–9.
26 Andrew Critchlow, Opec refuses to cut oil production, prices slump to five-year low. *Telegraph*, 27 November 2014.
27 See a report of Khamenei's comments in: Khamenei says Iraq can battle IS without foreigners. *The Daily Star*, 21 October 2014.
28 Iranian air force bombs Isis targets in Iraq, says Pentagon. *Guardian*, 3 December 2014.

Chapter 6   Conclusion

1 For details, see Jeffrey Goldberg, The crisis in US–Israeli relations is officially here. *The Atlantic*, 28 October 2014.

References

Abrahamian, Ervand. *Iran Between Two Revolutions.* Princeton: Princeton University Press, 1982.

Abrahamian, Ervand. *Khomeinism: Essays on the Islamic Republic.* London: I. B. Tauris, 1993.

Afary, Janet. *The Iranian Constitutional Revolution, 1906–1911: Grassroots Democracy, Social Democracy, and the Origins of Feminism.* New York: Columbia University Press, 1996.

Algar, Hamid. *Religion and State in Iran, 1785–1906: The Role of the Ulama in the Qajar Period.* Berkeley: University of California Press, 1969.

Amid, Javad. The dilemma of cheap food and self-sufficiency: The case of wheat in Iran. *Food Policy* 32(4) 2007, 537–52.

Amuzegar, Jahangir. Iran's economy in turmoil. *Carnegie Endowment for International Peace.* 18 March 2010.

Amuzegar, Jahangir. *Iran's Economy under the Islamic Republic.* London: I. B. Tauris, 1993.

Ansari, Ali M. Iran under Ahmadinejad: The politics of confrontation. *Adelphi Papers* 47/393. Abingdon: Routledge for the International Institute for Strategic Studies, 2007.

Ansari, Ali M. *Modern Iran Since 1921: The Pahlavis and After.* London: Longman, 2003.

159

References

Arjomand, Said Amir. *After Khomeini: Iran under His Successors*. Oxford: Oxford University Press, 2009.

Arjomand, Said Amir. *The Turban for the Crown: The Islamic Revolution in Iran*. Oxford: Oxford University Press, 1988.

Askari, Hossein. Iran's slide to the bottom. *Asia Times Online*, 15 September 2010, available at: www.atimes.com/atimes/Middle_East/LI15Ako1.html.

Axworthy, Michael. *Iran: Empire of the Mind: A History from Zoroaster to the Present Day*. London: Penguin, 2008.

Bahgat, Gawdat. Nuclear proliferation: The Islamic Republic of Iran. *Iranian Studies* 39(3) 2006, 307–27.

Bani Sadr, Abol-Hassan. *My Turn to Speak: Iran, the Revolution and Secret Deals with the US*. New York: Brassey's, 1991.

BBC News (Persian edition). 26 July 2014, available at: www.bbc.co.uk/persian/iran/2014/07/140726_ran_rouhani_friday_prayer_qods_day.

Behrooz, Maziar. Factionalism in Iran under Khomeini. *Middle Eastern Studies* 27(4) 1991, 597–614.

Bill, James A. *The Eagle and the Lion: The Tragedy of American-Iranian Relations*. New Haven, CT: Yale University Press, 1988.

Blight, James G., Lang, Janet M., Banai, Hussein, Byrne, Malcolm and Tirman, John. *Becoming Enemies: US–Iran Relations and the Iran–Iraq War, 1979–1988*. Lanham, MD: Rowman & Littlefield, 2012.

Booth, William. Israel's Netanyahu calls Iran deal 'historic mistake'. *Washington Post*, 24 November 2013.

Borger, Julian. Khamenei's son takes control of Iran's anti-protest militia. *Guardian*, 8 July 2009.

Briant, Pierre. *From Cyrus to Alexander: A History of the Persian Empire*. Winona Lake, IN: Eisenbrauns, 2002.

Brzezinski, Zbigniew, Scowcroft, Brent and Murphy,

References

Richard. Differentiated containment. *Foreign Affairs* 76(3) 1997, 20–30.

Burke, Jason. Riyadh will build nuclear weapons if Iran gets them, Saudi prince warns. *Guardian*, 29 June 2011.

Bush's 'evil axis' comment stirs critics. *BBC News*, 2 February 2002.

Carter, Jimmy. Tehran, Iran Toasts of the President and the Shah at a State Dinner. 31 December 1977, available at: *The American Presidency Project*. www.presidency.ucsb. edu/ws/?pid=7080.

Critchlow, Andrew. Opec refuses to cut oil production, prices slump to five-year low. *Telegraph*, 27 November 2014.

'Cut off head of snake', Saudis told US on Iran. *Reuters*, 29 November 2010.

Dobbins, James. Negotiating with Iran: Reflections from personal experience. *Washington Quarterly* 33(1) 2010, 149–62.

Drug addiction in Iran: The other religion. *The Economist*, 17 August 2013.

Eberling, George G. *Future Oil Demands of China, India, and Japan: Policy Scenarios and Implications*. Lanham, MD: Lexington Books, 2014.

Ehteshami, Anoushirvan, *After Khomeini: The Iranian Second Republic*, London: Taylor & Francis, 2002.

Ehteshami, Anoushirvan and Zweiri, Mahjoob. *Iran and the Rise of Its Neoconservatives: The Politics of Tehran's Silent Revolution*. London: I. B. Tauris, 2007.

Einhorn, Robert. A justified extension for Iran nuclear talks, but hard choices ahead. Brookings, 19 July 2014, available at: www.brookings.edu/blogs/iran-at-saban/posts/2014/07/19-iran-nuclear-talks-extended-hard-choices-enrichment.

Enayat, Hamid. Iran: Khumayni's concept of the 'Guardianship of the Jurisconsult'. In: Piscatori, James P.

References

(ed.), *Islam in the Political Process*. New York: Cambridge University Press, 1983, pp. 160–80.

Erdbrink, Thomas. Iranian leader rebuffs Ahmadinejad over official's dismissal. *Washington Post*, 20 April 2011.

Esposito, John L. (ed.) *The Oxford Encyclopedia of the Modern Islamic World*, vol. 1. Oxford: Oxford University Press, 1995.

Farber, David. *Taken Hostage: The Iran Hostage Crisis and America's First Encounter with Radical Islam*. Princeton: Princeton University Press, 2005.

Fleishman, Jeffrey. Iran Supreme Leader's son seen as power broker with big ambitions. *Los Angeles Times*, 25 June 2009.

Foreign investors in Iran growing: Official. *Islamic Republic News Agency*, 5 November 2014, available at: www.irna.ir/en/News/2783563/.

Friedman, Alan. *Spider's Web: The Secret History of How the White House Illegally Armed Iraq*. New York: Bantam Books, 1993.

Gates, Robert. *Duty: Memoirs of a Secretary at War*. New York: Alfred A. Knopf, 2014.

Gause III, F. Gregory. The illogic of dual containment. *Foreign Affairs* 73(2) 1994, 56–66.

Goldberg, Jeffrey. The crisis in US–Israeli relations is officially here. *The Atlantic*, 28 October 2014.

Hargreaves, Steve. Iraq oil production surpasses Iran. *CNN Money*, 10 August 2012.

Harrison, Frances. Huge cost of Iranian brain drain. *BBC News*, 8 January 2007.

Heiss, Mary Ann. *Empire and Nationhood: The United States, Great Britain, and Iranian Oil, 1950–1954*. New York: Columbia University Press, 1997.

Hen-Tov, Elliot. Understanding Iran's new authoritarianism. *Washington Quarterly* 30(1) 2006–7, 163–79.

References

Hiro, Dilip. *The Longest War: The Iran–Iraq Military Conflict*. London: Grafton, 1989.

Houghton, David Patrick. *US Foreign Policy and the Iran Hostage Crisis*. Cambridge: Cambridge University Press, 2001.

Hunter, Jane. Israeli arms sales to Iran. *Washington Report on Middle East Affairs*, November 1986.

Hunter, Shireen T. Iran and the spread of revolutionary Islam. *Third World Quarterly* 10(2) 1988, 730–49.

Hunter, Shireen T. *Iran's Foreign Policy in the Post-Soviet Era: Resisting the New International Order*. Santa Barbara, CA: Praeger, 2010.

Hunter, Shireen T. Islamic reformist discourse in Iran. In: Hunter, Shireen T. (ed.), *Reformist Voices of Islam: Mediating Islam and Modernity*. New York: Routledge, 2009, pp. 33–97.

IISS (International Institute for Strategic Studies). *The Military Balance 2014*. London: Routledge, 2014.

India oil imports from Iran jump sharply in 2014. *Economic Times*, 16 January 2015.

International Crisis Group. *Iran: The Struggle for the Revolution's Soul*. Middle East Report No. 5, 5 August 2002.

Iran plans to tax religious foundations, army-linked firms. *The Daily Star*, 4 December 2014.

Iran to hike military spending despite 'tight' budget. *World Bulletin*, 8 December 2014.

Iranian air force bombs Isis targets in Iraq, says Pentagon. *Guardian*, 3 December 2014.

Iran's Rouhani calls Israel 'old wound' on Islamic world. *BBC News*, 2 August 2013.

Jahanbegloo, Ramin. The two sovereignties and the legitimacy crisis in Iran. *Constellations* 17(1) 2010, 22–30.

Karsh, Efraim. *The Iran–Iraq War: 1980–1988*. Oxford: Osprey Publishing, 2002.

References

Karshenas, Massoud and Hakimian, Hassan. Managing oil resources and economic diversification in Iran. In: Katouzian, Homa and Shahidi, Hossein (eds), *Iran in the 21st Century: Politics, Economics and Conflict*. Abingdon, Oxon: Routledge, 2008, pp. 194–216.

Katouzian, Homa. *The Persians: Ancient, Mediaeval and Modern Iran*. New Haven, CT: Yale University Press, 2009.

Katz, Mark N. Why Russia won't play ball on Iran. *The Diplomat*, 23 June 2012.

Kazemzadeh, Firuz. *Russia and Britain in Persia: Imperial Ambitions in Qajar Iran*. New Haven, CT: Yale University Press, 2013.

Khamenei says Iraq can battle IS without foreigners. *The Daily Star*, 21 October 2014.

Khatami, Mohammad. *Dialogue and the New Millennium*. Address Delivered to the Thirtieth General Conference of the United Nations Educational Scientific and Cultural Organization (UNESCO), Paris. 29 October 1999.

Khatami, Mohammad. *Islam, Dialogue and Civil Society*. Canberra: Centre for Arab and Islamic Studies, Australian National University, 2000.

Khomeini, Ayatollah Ruhollah. *Islamic Government*. Springfield, VA: National Technical Information Service, 1979.

Kinzer, Stephen. *All the Shah's Men: An American Coup and the Roots of Middle East Terror*. Hoboken, NJ: John Wiley & Sons, 2003.

Kissinger, Henry. *World Order: Reflections on the Character of Nations and the Course of History*. New York: Allen Lane, 2014.

Klebnikov, Paul. Millionaire mullahs. *Forbes*, 21 July 2003.

Kuniholm, Bruce R. *The Origins of the Cold War in the Near East: Great Power Conflict and Diplomacy in Iran, Turkey, and Greece*. Princeton: Princeton University Press, 1980.

References

Limbert, John. The Obama administration. In: Wright, Robin (ed.), *The Iran Primer: Power, Politics, and US Policy*. Washington, DC: United States Institute of Peace Press, 2010, pp. 146–8.

Lucas, Scott. Blow to Rouhani as parliament dismisses science minister. *EA World View*, 21 August 2014.

Lucas, Scott. Rouhani makes a play for support with public votes – but on which issues? *EA Worldview*, 6 January 2015.

Maloney, Suzanne. Agents or obstacles? Parastatal foundations and challenges for Iranian development. In: Alizadeh, Parvin (ed.), *The Economy of Iran: The Dilemmas of an Islamic State*. London: I. B. Tauris, 2000, pp. 145–76.

Matthee, Rudi. *Persia in Crisis: Safavid Decline and the Fall of Isfahan*. London: I. B. Tauris, 2012.

Merat, Arron. Rouhani deals with Ahmadinejad's economic legacy. *Al Monitor*, 11 September 2013, available at: www.al-monitor.com/pulse/fr/originals/2013/09/ahmadinejad-leaves-rouhani-economic-problems.html.

Michel, David. Iran's environment: Greater threat than foreign foes. United States Institute of Peace, 28 October 2013, available at: iranprimer.usip.org/blog/2013/oct/28/iran%E2%80%99s-environment-greater-threat-foreign-foes.

Milani, Abbas. *Eminent Persians: The Men and Women Who Made Modern Iran, 1941–1979*, vol. 1. New York: Syracuse University Press, 2008.

Mirsepassi, Ali. *Democracy in Modern Iran: Islam, Culture, and Political Change*. New York: New York University Press, 2010.

Moin, Baqer. *Khomeini: Life of the Ayatollah*. London: I. B. Tauris, 1999.

Moore, Heidi. Sanctions are pushing Iran towards nuclear talks, just not US sanctions. *Guardian*, 24 October 2012.

References

Moslem, Mehdi. *Factional Politics in Post-Khomeini Iran.* New York: Syracuse University Press, 2002.

Mossadeq, Mohammad. *Mossadeq's Memoirs,* trans. S. H. Amin and H. Katouzian. London: JEBHE, National Movement of Iran, 1988.

Motevalli, Golnar. Rouhani: Iran budget to face short-term pressure from oil. *The Daily Star,* 8 December 2014.

Naji, Kasra. *Ahmadinejad: The Secret History of Iran's Radical Leader.* Berkeley: University of California Press, 2008.

Nasr, Vali. *The Shia Revival: How Conflicts within Islam Will Shape the Future.* New York: W. W. Norton & Co., 2006.

National Commission on Terrorist Attacks Upon the United States. The 9/11 Commission Report. 22 July 2004, available at: www.9-11commission.gov/report/.

Nirumand, Bahman. *Iran: The New Imperialism in Action,* trans. Leonard Mins. New York: Monthly Review Press, 1969.

Norton, Augustus Richard. *Hezbollah: A Short History.* Princeton: Princeton University Press, 2007.

Office of the Press Secretary. Videotape remarks by the President in celebration of Nowruz. 20 March 2009, available at: www.youtube.com/watch?v=HY_utC-hrjI.

Pahlavi, Mohammad Reza Shah. *Answer to History.* Toronto: Irwin & Co., 1980.

Pahlavi, Mohammad Reza Shah. *Mission for My Country.* New York: McGraw Hill, 1961.

Pahlavi, Mohammad Reza. *Towards the Great Civilization,* in Persian. Tehran: Pahlavi Library Publication, 1977.

Parsi, Trita. *Treacherous Alliance: The Secret Dealings of Israel, Iran, and the United States.* New Haven, CT: Yale University Press, 2007.

Patrikarakos, David. *Nuclear Iran: The Birth of an Atomic State.* London: I. B. Tauris, 2012.

References

Pelletiere, Stephen C. *The Iran–Iraq War: Chaos in a Vacuum*. New York: Praeger, 1992.

Pesaran, Evaleila. *Iran's Struggle for Economic Independence: Reform and Counter-Reform in the Post-Revolutionary Era*. New York: Routledge, 2011.

Pollack, Kenneth M. *The Persian Puzzle: The Conflict Between Iran and America*. New York: Random House, 2004.

Pourshariati, Parvaneh. *Decline and Fall of the Sasanian Empire: The Sasanian-Parthian Confederacy and the Arab Conquest of Iran*. London: I. B. Tauris, 2008.

Rajaee, Bahram. Deciphering Iran: The political evolution of the Islamic Republic and US foreign policy after September 11. *Comparative Studies of South Asia, Africa and the Middle East* 24(1) 2004, 159–72.

Rakel, Eva. Conglomerates in Iran: The political economy of Islamic foundations. In: Jilberto, Alex E. Fernández and Hogenboom, Barbara (eds), *Big Business and Economic Development: Conglomerates and Economic Groups in Developing Countries and Transition Economies under Globalisation*. New York: Routledge, 2007, pp. 109–32.

Rakel, Eva Patricia. The political elite in the Islamic Republic of Iran: From Khomeini to Ahmadinejad. *Comparative Studies of South Asia, Africa and the Middle East* 29(1) 2009, 105–25.

Ramazani, R. K. Iran's foreign policy: Contending orientations. *Middle East Journal* 43(2) 1989, 202–17.

Rezalan, Jason. Iran's Supreme Leader, Ayatollah Ali Khamenei, endorses diplomacy over militarism. *Washington Post*, 17 September 2013.

Rouhani, Hassan. *Rawaiti-e Tadbir wa Omid* [Narration of Foresight and Hope]. Tehran: Center for Strategic Research, 2013.

Saeidi, Ali A. The accountability of para-governmental

organizations (*bonyads*): The case of Iranian foundations. *Iranian Studies* 37(3) 2004, 479–98.

Saikal, Amin. Afghanistan's geographic possibilities. *Survival: Global Politics and Strategy* 56(3) 2014, 141–56.

Saikal, Amin. Iraq: Elite fragmentation, Islam and democracy. In: Akbarzadeh, Shahram, MacQueen, Benjamin, Piscatori, James, and Saikal, Amin (eds), *American Democracy Promotion in the Changing Middle East: From Bush to Obama*. London: Routledge, 2013, pp. 101–13.

Saikal, Amin. *Islam and the West: Conflict or Cooperation?* London: Palgrave Macmillan, 2003.

Saikal, Amin. Islamism, the Iranian revolution, and the Soviet invasion of Afghanistan. In: Leffler, Melvyn P. and Westad, Odd Arne (eds), *The Cambridge History of the Cold War*. Vol. 3: *Endings*. Cambridge: Cambridge University Press, 2009, pp. 112–34.

Saikal, Amin. Kemalism: Its influences on Iran and Afghanistan. *International Journal of Turkish Studies* 2(2) 1982, 25–32.

Saikal, Amin. The politics of factionalism in Iran. Workshop paper in Green, Jerrod D., Wehrey, Frederic and Wolf Jr, Charles (eds), *Understanding Iran*. Santa Monica, CA: RAND, 2009, pp. 96–104.

Saikal, Amin. The promises of a US-Iranian rapprochement. *ABC News Australia*, 25 November 2013.

Saikal, Amin. *The Rise and Fall of the Shah: Iran from Autocracy to Religious Rule*. Princeton: Princeton University Press, 2009.

Saikal, Amin. The roots of Iran's election crisis. *Survival: Global Politics and Strategy* 51(5) 2009, 91–104.

Saikal, Amin. The United States and Persian Gulf security. *World Policy Journal* 9(3) 1992, 515–31.

Saikal, Amin. *Zone of Crisis: Afghanistan, Pakistan, Iran and Iraq*. London: I. B. Tauris, 2014.

References

Samii, Abbas William. The Iranian nuclear issue and informal networks. *Naval War College Review* 59(1) 2006, 63–89.

Sandbrook, Dominic. After the revolution. *New Statesman*, 16 June 2009.

Savory, Roger. *Iran Under the Safavids.* Cambridge: Cambridge University Press, 1980.

Schirazi, Asghar. *The Constitution of Iran: Politics and the State in the Islamic Republic.* London: I. B. Tauris, 1998.

Sciolino, Elaine. Iran offers trade on hostages, but US is cautious. *New York Times*, 24 October 1989.

Sick, Gary. *All Fall Down: America's Tragic Encounter with Iran.* New York: Random House, 1985.

Takeyh, Ray. *Hidden Iran: Paradox and Power in the Islamic Republic.* New York: Times Books, 2006.

Tarock, Adam. Iran–Western Europe relations on the mend. *British Journal of Middle Eastern Studies* 26(1) 1999, 41–61.

Torchia, Andrew. Politics, markets complicate Rouhani's rescue of Iran economy. *Reuters*, 1 May 2014.

Transparency International. Corruption by country/territory: Iran, available at: www.transparency.org/country#IRN.

Warnaar, Maaike. *Iranian Foreign Policy during Ahmadinejad: Ideology and Actions.* New York: Palgrave Macmillan, 2013.

World Bank. Iran country brief. September 2010, available at: siteresources.worldbank.org/INTIRAN/Resources/Iran_Web_brief.pdf.

World Bank. Iran overview, available at: www.worldbank.org/en/country/iran/overview.

Wroe, Ann. *Lives, Lies and the Iran-Contra Affair.* London: I. B. Tauris, 1992.

Zonis, Marvin. *The Political Elite of Iran.* Princeton: Princeton University Press, 1971.

Index

Index

Index

Index

Index

Index

175

Index

Index

177

Index

Index

Index

Index